"I have observed how the grip of materialism can strangle a person and an organization. The only cure is understanding and applying God's principles of stewardship and generosity. It's all there in the Bible. Money DOES Matter. Learn from Mike, one of the best teachers of our time, about how to get in sync with God's game plan."

—Bob Buford, Founding Chairman, Leadership Network

Other Books by Michael Slaughter

Spiritual Entrepreneurs: Six Principles for Risking Renewal

Out on the Edge: A Wakeup Call for Church Leaders on the Edge of the Media Reformation

Real Followers: Beyond Virtual Christianity

UnLearning Church: Transforming Spiritual Leadership for the Emerging Church

Momentum for Life: Sustaining Personal Health, Integrity, and Strategic Focus As A Leader

MONEY MATTERS

Financial Freedom for All God's Children

Michael Slaughter

with

Kim Miller

Abingdon Press

Nashville

Library of Congress Cataloging-in-Publication Data

Slaughter, Michael.

Money Matters : financial freedom for all God's children / Michael Slaughter with Kim Miller.

p. cm.

ISBN 0-687-49535-0

1. Wealth—Religious aspects—Christianity. 2. Finance, Personal—Religious aspects—Christianity. I. Miller, Kim, 1956- II. Title.

Unless otherwise noted, Scripture references are from *The Holy Bible: Today's New International Version* (TNIV), © 2001, 2005 by The International Bible Society. Used by permission.

Scripture references marked NRSV are from *The New Revised Standard Version*, © 1989 by The National Council of Churches of Christ. Used by permission.

06 07 08 09 10 11 12 13 14 15—10 09 08 07 06 05 04 03 02 01

MANUFACTURED IN THE UNITED STATES OF AMERICA

This book is dedicated to the faithful stewards of

Ginghamsburg Church who are faithfully practicing

the disciplines of financial freedom for the

purpose of courageously serving

the needs of the world that God loves.

Acknowledgements

I thank:

My wife Carolyn for being a model of faithful stewardship and sacrifice in serving the needs of others in the mission of Jesus Christ.

Kim Miller (Creative Director of Ginghamsburg Church) for her incredible gift of making my work better.

My editor Paul Franklyn and his team at Abingdon Press, for encouraging this project that I might not have otherwise written.

The people of Ginghamsburg Church who powerfully demonstrate the presence and power of Jesus through sacrificial giving and servant living.

Foreword

Each year as the Christmas season draws near, I am reminded that Christmas is not my birthday. Christmas is Jesus' birthday. The true Light that came into the world to bring hope and liberation to all people continues to shine brightly through real followers today. As disciples of Jesus, we are his hands and feet to take justice and hope to the lost and oppressed.

Materialism and debt continue to be one of the major oppressive forces that keep people from living fully as sons and daughters of God. We are created in the image of God and are never closer to God than when meeting the real needs of people. *"Truly I tell you, whatever you did for one of the least of these brothers and sisters of mine, you did for me"* (Matthew 25:40). My prayer is for you to know the joy of financial freedom and the amazing abundance of generous living.

Mike Slaughter

January 2006

Contents

Part One

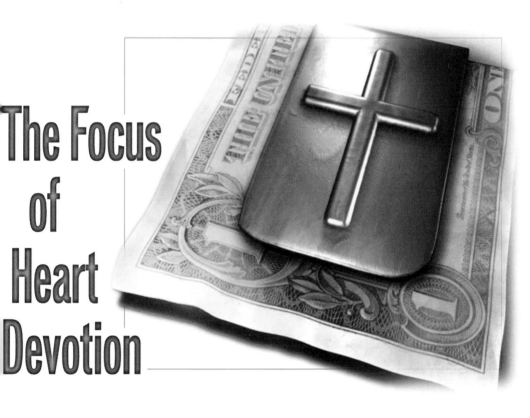

The Focus
of
Heart
Devotion

"Take hold
of the life
that is
truly life..."

Chapter One

A Faith-filled Focus

Command those who are rich in this present world not to be arrogant nor to put their hope in wealth, which is so uncertain, but to put their hope in God, who richly provides us with everything for our enjoyment. Command them to do good, to be rich in good deeds, and to be generous and willing to share. In this way they will lay up treasure for themselves as a firm foundation for the coming age, so that they may take hold of the life that is truly life—
1 Timothy 6:17-19

Money matters, doesn't it? While television evangelists have long-abused the word *prosperity*, it is still true that God desires success for all God's children. I am passionately convinced that every person will experience transformation in their life when they put their faith into action by practicing the timeless principles addressed in this book.

Think about how much of your energy each week is tied in some way to money. The prime time of our days and weeks is given to earning money. Every day you make numerous financial decisions. Everything costs money, from food for your family, to gas for your car, to the roof over your head.

Our finances are unstable at best, because every part of our life is tied to economic forces that are much bigger than any individual. Consider the impact of September 11, 2001, the day that a war began, when so much changed. It was the official end to the boom of the 1990s, during which the economy grew rapidly and the stock market appreciated at a reckless pace. The average person lost 40 percent of his or her financial investments or retirement funds as a result of 9/11.

Beyond the hard facts about our finances, money matters take an emotional toll on our lives and in our relationships. The Gallup Poll verifies that 56 percent of all divorces are the result of financial tension.

All God's children can be free from financial worry, however, because God gives us biblical principles to open the doors to financial freedom. Whether as debt-ridden adults or credit-tempted students, there can be no better time than right now to experience transformation in our money matters.

Powerful Parent

As we build a platform for wealth in every sense of the term, we should begin with the understanding that we have a powerful parent. If you and I as humans are willing to go to such great lengths to be with and provide for our children, how much more God? This parental promise is what Jesus implied in Matthew 7:7-11:

> Ask and you will receive; seek and you will find; knock and the door will be opened for you. Is there anyone among you who, if your child asks for bread, will give a stone? Or if the child asks for a fish, will give a snake? If you then, who are evil, know how to give good gifts to your children, how much more will your Father in heaven give good things to those who ask him! (NRSV)

I had a toy not too long ago, a 1960 Corvette with silver coves, a white soft top, and nine perfect chrome teeth in the front. There is a special connection between men and their toys. Often I'll call a friend's house and his wife will answer the phone and tell me that my friend is out in the garage. Women seldom go out to the garage just to look at their car or motorcycle or whatever's out there, but men can be caught just opening the door and sighing!

The number one question I'm asked is, "Why don't you have your Corvette anymore? What happened to the car?" Only one thing could cause me to **The heart of a parent does** give up that car: a child, a child who **whatever is required for the** needed to attend college. And here's the **sake of the child.** sad thing: I'll probably never be able to buy another Corvette because already that car is worth three times what I paid for it. I knew when I let it go that I was letting it go for good, but the heart of a parent does whatever is required for the sake of the child.

Notice the authority of Jesus' teaching, because Matthew is very inten-tional: *"your Father in heaven."* That's not merely a title; it's a position. God is in the all-powerful position to back you with all the resources of heaven. God is in the position to back God's promises. I saw how this analogy works when a family friend from our church was in Philadelphia and called my son's apartment to take Jonathan out to supper. This man wanted to stop by the college bookstore on the way to the restaurant to buy his wife a University of Pennsylvania sweatshirt. The three of them went to the bookstore to buy it, and Jonathan said, "You don't have to worry about paying for that. We'll just put it on my bursar account and let my dad pay for it." It didn't matter that my son had no resources to his name, because Jonathan knew that his father was in a position to back him!

> *"Indeed, the very hairs of your head are all numbered. Don't be afraid; you are worth more than many sparrows."—Jesus, Luke 12:7*

There are many things you can control in your life, but ironically you have no control over God's love for you. There is nothing you can do to change God's love, no matter how badly you mess up. Jesus told us that God even has *the hairs on your head numbered*—he knows the exact number. If an earthly father would get involved with a passion for a a piece of steel that was made in 1960, only to give it up for his child, how much more your heavenly father?

The Promise of Provision

THE PROMISE OF PROVISION

As we're building a platform of financial freedom into our lives, the amazing truth is that we not only have a powerful parent, we have a powerful parent who has given us the promise of provision. *"And my God will meet all your needs according to his glorious riches in Christ Jesus"* (Philippians 4:19).

The Bible offers one narrative after another that illustrates how no need is too great for God to meet. When the Israelites were out in the middle of the desert without anything to eat, God provided manna and quail. When

There is nothing you can do to change God's love, no matter how badly you mess up.

there was nothing to drink, God pulled water out of a rock. When the only available resources to feed 5,000 people were a few dry fish and five loaves of bread, Jesus multiplied them to feed the multitudes. *"He who did not spare his own Son but gave him up for us all—how will he not also, along with him, graciously give us all things?"* (Romans 8:32) If God was willing to give Jesus to die for you, does not everything else pale in comparison to Love's ability to provide for your every need?

Financial freedom is based in trust; that is, in building a trusting relationship between you and God. Life is not about frantically pursuing money and possessions, because God's already promised all we need. Life is about pursuing a relationship with God the Father through Jesus Christ. We begin to build a lifetime of financial freedom by readjusting our priorities. Jesus put it this way: **But strive first for the kingdom of God and his righteousness, and all these things will be given to you as well.** *"But strive first for the kingdom of God and his righteousness, and all these things will be given to you as well."*—Matthew 6:33 NRSV. I don't have to worry about multiplying wealth because God has promised that to me. All I need worry about is staying in a right relationship with God, making sure that God is first.

The Principle of Biblical Prosperity

I don't know any parents who want their children to make average grades in school, who hope their kids will struggle their way through life, and who dream of their children growing up to be poor. All parents desire the best for their children, and our heavenly parent is no different. Despite the fact that God loves you and has promised to abundantly meet all of your needs, financial freedom is not going to merely "happen." Thinking that success comes solely by being under God's covering or protection is one of the biggest mistakes that the people of God can make. In the Old Testament, the Israelites sometimes felt that they were blessed just because they are the children of Abraham.

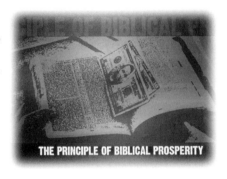

THE PRINCIPLE OF BIBLICAL PROSPERITY

As Christians we also often make the mistake of expecting that we're going to be blessed just because we're redeemed by the blood of Jesus Christ. **As Christians we also often make the mistake of expecting that we're going to be blessed just because we're redeemed by the blood of Jesus Christ.** No, we must submit ourselves to all of the laws and principles of God. Ephesians 5:17 says *"Do not be foolish but understand what the LORD's will is."* You must understand the will of the Lord and submit yourself to it. This is the beginning of developing a healthy biblical perspective about wealth.

Today Is the Day

We declare that today is the day of our salvation, and we keep our focus upon the devotion of our heart. We remember that we have a powerful parent, a father who is in heaven. What are parents willing to do for the success of their children? To what extent are parents willing to go? Jesus taught us to pray, *Our Father, who art in heaven*, because Jesus is in the position of power and authority, which means that he can back his promises. We have a father in heaven who has promised to provide us everything we need. In Jesus Christ we have all of the resources needed for financial freedom. In Jesus every promise of God for our success is "yes!"

Further Steps For Freedom Finders

It All Matters:

1. **Consider your earthly parents.** How were they similar or different than your powerful heavenly parent?

2. **Do you truly believe that "there is nothing you can do to change God's love, no matter how badly you mess up"?** Financial freedom will come only as we accept God's love, care, and provision for us as God's children.

Devoted to Our Rightful Owner

*Moses answered, "What if they do not believe me or listen to me and say, 'The L*ORD* did not appear to you'?"*

*Then the L*ORD* said to him, "What is that in your hand?"*

"A staff," he replied.

*The L*ORD* said, "Throw it on the ground."*

*Moses threw it on the ground and it became a snake, and he ran from it. Then the L*ORD* said to him, "Reach out your hand and take it by the tail." So Moses reached out and took hold of the snake and it turned back into a staff in his hand.*

*"This," said the L*ORD*, "is so that they may believe that the L*ORD*, the God of their fathers—the God of Abraham, the God of Isaac and the God of Jacob—has appeared to you."*

*Then the L*ORD* said, "Put your hand inside your cloak." So Moses put his hand into his cloak, and when he took it out, it was leprous, like snow.*

"Now put it back into your cloak," he said. So Moses put his hand back into his cloak, and when he took it out, it was restored, like the rest of his flesh.

*Then the L*ORD* said, "If they do not believe you or pay attention to the first miraculous sign, they may believe the second. But if they do not believe these two signs or listen to you, take some water from the Nile and pour it on the dry ground. The water you take from the river will become blood on the ground."*

Moses said to the Lord, "Pardon your servant, Lord. I have never been eloquent, neither in the past nor since you have spoken to your servant. I am slow of speech and tongue."

*The L*ORD* said to him, "Who gives human beings their mouth? Who makes them deaf or mute? Who gives them sight or makes them blind? Is it not I, the L*ORD*? Now go; I will help you speak and will teach you what to say."—Exodus 4:1-12*

God's intention and aggressive purpose in each of our lives is for freedom in every aspect. Sometimes it is hard to see how our financial situation is of concern to God. We tend to put God and spiritual matters in one compartment, and our financial situation in another, separating the two. The truth is, however, that God is more concerned about your financial freedom than you are. A vast number of passages in the Scripture describe God's promise of provision and God's intent for physical blessing in our lives. Consider how many of Jesus' miracles were physical. Jesus wasn't just about saving people for heaven later; Jesus' ministry was about creating freedom and health for lives on earth.

God is more concerned about your financial freedom than you are. A great percentage of Jesus' teachings were about money and possessions. Twenty-seven out of forty-three parables in the Bible are metaphors for the subject of money. The Bible asserts that *the love of money is a root of all kinds of evil.* It doesn't say that possessing money is the root of all evil; rather the wrong focus and corrupt financial practices will define the evil.

A Series of Conversions

I believe that there is one new birth in life, which is the time when a person accepts Jesus Christ as Lord and Savior and the Holy Spirit comes into his or her life, making available all the resources of heaven. There seems to be one new birth, but each of us will likely experience a series of conversions throughout a lifetime. Conversion is a point at which you have a change of thinking and a change of practice in any specific area of your life. As you learn and practice spiritual discipline, you change your thinking and behavior to conform to the perspective and renewing action of Jesus.

Conversion is a point at which you have a change of thinking and a change of practice in any specific area of your life. By analogy, when Carolyn and I got married we had both experienced the new birth. We both had all the resources of heaven and the Holy Spirit. But we did not reach our potential during the first twenty years of marriage because we had not yet converted our practices into the type of marriage that God promises. We needed to practice God's perspective of marriage before the resources of the Holy Spirit could be released for God's blessings in our relationship. We were sitting on those resources for twenty years until our relational conversion.

As another example many of us presently are slaves financially. We have been born again and have all the resources of the Holy Spirit in our lives, but the resources cannot be released until we are converted. Conversion in our finances means we will change our thinking and practice to the thinking and practice of Jesus. Carolyn and I were converted financially when we married, and these financial principles have been working in our lives since day one; we didn't waste any time in this area. We have experienced the multiplication and blessing of financial freedom in our lives for more than thirty years. Remember, God is still in the conversion business even after you have accepted God's love. As you read this book you may experience a financial conversion!

The Recognition of Rightful Ownership

Financial freedom requires the recognition that God is the rightful owner of all things. Exodus 4:2 depicts God calling Moses to a place of conversion, to a higher place in his life. God asked Moses a great question.

The LORD said to him, "What is that in your hand?" Moses said, "It's a staff." For Moses, the staff represented the tool of his trade as a shepherd. It repre-

sented his skills and talents and all of his experience, which is the package that God had given him to make a living and a life. Everything Moses needed for financial freedom and to fulfill God's purpose was already in his hand.

We typically use credit cards for what's not in our hand. We believe that to find freedom and life purpose we need something that we don't already have; we get into debt to acquire something that's not in our hand. The only thing God is going to bless supernaturally for his purpose is what you are already holding in your hand.

This is why the Bible asserts that debt is bad. Debt is not our friend. Now, you are saying, "What if I had more of… if I only had this… if I only had a different job." This kind of thinking is self-defeating, because you already have everything you need. God has given you talent, skill, and experience to move you towards freedom.

I only brought one skill to the table. I wasn't a good student or athlete. I wasn't even a great musician, but I apparently exhibited the gift of bull. It was amazing how I could talk myself (and others) out of all kinds of negative situations. (Do not try this at home; this behavior was characteristic during my lost days.) In third grade, my friend and I were down by the creek smoking. Mrs. Osterwich, who lived on my street, saw Jeff and me smoking down by the creek, so she called my father. My father was waiting with his belt off when I got home. (Parents, do not imitate this at home; this occurred during in my dad's lost days.) My dad said, "You were smoking down by the creek." I said, "Dad, we were lighting leaves, letting them float in the water, and throwing rocks at them. Mrs. Osterwich must have seen the smoke from the leaves!"

My dad bought it! That's what I mean by the gift of "bull." My dad would say to me, "That smooth talk is not going to get you anywhere." What you have in your hand, God has given you. And when it is redeemed through the new birth and released through the conversion of faith, even the gift of bull can become a leadership tool.

You may be thinking, "I'm a janitor; I have a broomstick in my hand. What can I do with a broomstick?" Perhaps you have heard of Famous Amos or eaten one of his deadly cookies? Wally Amos was a janitor, but he liked to bake cookies. He would give them to people at work. Someone said to him, "You know what you ought to do with these cookies?" And Wally Amos did it! He started a wildly successful cookie company, and has gone on to write books and speak to large audiences about the positive values he believes in. Now Wally is famous and financially free!

You already have in your hands everything you need for financial freedom. Don't see who you are or what you have as a liability? Moses did. Moses said to the Lord: *"Oh Lord, I have never been eloquent, neither in the past* **You already have in your** *nor even now that you have spoken to* **hands everything you need** *your servant. I am slow of speech and* **for financial freedom.** *slow of tongue."* Moses stuttered. He saw himself as a liability. But in God's hand, he was an asset. So, the Lord said to him, *"Who gives human beings their mouth? Who makes them deaf or mute?"* Here is the only asset we need: *"Now go; I will help you speak and will teach you what to say."* Our greatest hope is that who we are and what we are represent our greatest gifts from God.

The Responsibility of Trust

How much of whom we are and what we are belongs to God? Everything. Sometimes Christians make the mistake of thinking that the tithe (ten percent of our earned income) belongs to God and the ninety percent belongs to them, but that's where Christians get into trouble. The songwriter says, *"The earth is the LORD'S, and everything in it"* (Psalm 24:1). Everything belongs to God. Recognizing God's ownership is a critical step to financial freedom.

It is what Jesus meant when he said that no one can be his disciple who does not give up all their possessions. *"Go, sell everything you have and give to the poor, and you will have treasure in heaven. Then come, follow me"* (Mark 10:21). While this Scripture passage may trouble you, it doesn't mean that you must become poor and homeless; rather it exemplifies our responsibility to trust God for every need, and to give away what we don't need.

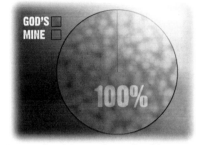

Meanwhile, back at the bush we hear God's question to Moses, *"What is that in your hand?"* (Exodus 4:3). Moses said, *"It's a staff."* The staff represents all Moses has, all of his gifts, all of his talents, everything he has collected in his lifetime, all of the resources he needs to make a living. He is expected to release it, for we must release it before God can increase it. God told Moses to throw his staff on the ground. In a similar response, God wants you to release what you have in your hand, not what you don't have. God isn't calling you to release what you *don't* have; he's calling you to release what you *do* have.

God isn't calling you to release what you *don't* have; he's calling you to release what you *do* have.

Anytime you go to a credit card and accrue interest on your purchases, you demonstrate a desire to possess something you do not have the means to possess. God's blessing can't be experienced by acquiring what you don't have but only by releasing what you do have. God will only bless and empower what you release to God's purpose.

Think about the miracles of Jesus. When Jesus performed a miracle, he always asked the recipient to release what they already had before he would multiply or increase it. Consider when he turned the water into wine? Remember, he lived in an arid desert country, and he asked the people to release the supply of water they stored in jugs by their front door. Water was a precious commodity in an arid, dry climate where there are no streams. They only had deep wells, requiring hard work to extract the water. You must release what you have in order for God to increase it. Remember when God multiplied the loaves and the fishes? All he could find was a child's lunch.

Jesus asked for the lunch, and when the boy released it Jesus increased it and fed thousands of people with an abundance left over. To give up all of your possessions means to claim ownership of nothing you have, to release everything to the hands of God. This is our demonstration of trust.

Belief vs. Faith

Many Christians talk about believing in Jesus, and perhaps subconsciously they avoid the term faith. Belief and *faith* are two very different things. I refuse to use the word *believer*. When you talk about a *believer*, you put the bar so low that it even includes Satan. Satan *believes* in Jesus. Many people say they believe in Jesus and they profess Jesus, but they put trust for their security and meaning in their physical possessions— from their money.

Many people say they believe in Jesus and they profess Jesus, but they put trust for their security and meaning in their physical possessions. From a Christian worldview, my security and my meaning do not come from my posses-sions or my money. My security and my meaning are derived from my relationship with God. God has a covenant with me through Jesus Christ. He will always provide for my every need when I activate that covenant through trust, not belief. Ultimately possessions can't give us meaning. Meaning comes from rela-tionships, and joy comes when I release the resources God has given me to create wellness in relationships.

You exhibit power with God by your actions toward other persons. If I'm in debt, how will I ever have resources to bless others, to love my neighbor as myself? God will only increase my power with people by my positive actions of releasing resources and creating health in the lives of others. We are the **You have power with God by your actions toward other persons.** body of Christ; we are the hands and feet of Jesus. If Jesus wants to bless somebody in the world, he is going to do so through our hands and feet. If Jesus is going to feed somebody in the world, he is going to do it through our hands and feet.

How can I do this? I trust God's love. That's different than believing in God's love. I trust God's intention toward me; I trust God's promise and provision. I recognize God's ownership, so I can release my resources to Jesus' Lordship. Not that I believe in his love, I trust his love. If Jesus is going to die for me, how much more is God willing to do? There is no concern that should worry me. None—because I trust God's provision and love, I recognize God's ownership and I release it to Jesus' Lordship.

What is in Your Hand?

Many times we wonder why some people seem to experience more blessing than others. (I am not addressing here why some people suffer more than others, which is a matter of injustice, rather than what you do with your talent. See the beginning of Chapter 3, and then Chapter 8, which explains the power of sacrifice.) God rewards faithfulness, and I say that without hesitation. There is a cause and effect relationship between people who are faithful with their resources and the increase of God's blessing and abundance in their

life. Matthew 25:19–23 includes the parable that Jesus told about the master who gave each of his servants a certain amount of talents. Remember that talent in your hand? You have everything you need; mine was the gift of bull, which God transformed into persuasion and passion. What do you do with that talent?

> *After a long time, the master of those servants returned and settled accounts with them.*

(God is going to return and settle accounts with all people.)

> *The man who had received five talents brought another five. "Master," he said, "you entrusted me with five talents; see I've gained five more." His master replied, "Well done, my good and faithful servant. Because you have been faithful with a few things, I will put you in charge of many things. Come and share your master's happiness."*

See how God works? When you are faithful with the little that God has entrusted you, God will increase it and reward you with more. If you aren't a good steward with a little, why do you think you deserve to be blessed with more? A conversion must take place in your life. You might have experienced the new birth. You might have the Holy Spirit in you. But the resources of the Spirit will not be released until you change from your thinking and practice to the thinking and practice of Jesus.

The reward for humility and fear of the Lord is riches and honor and life (Prov 22:4 NRSV).

Do you see the word *riches*? *"Humility and fear of the Lord"* is about agreeing with the Lord and changing from your thinking and practice

The resources of the Spirit will not be released until you change to the thinking and practice of Jesus. financially to the thinking and practice of Jesus. You no longer hear the voice of God and do the opposite. For example, if God says tithe and you're not tithing, you are saying to God, "God, listen. Let me try to convince you that my worldview is better than yours." You're not going to win that one! Not only are you not going to win that one, financially you are going to live like I lived for twenty years, with God saying, "Okay, as soon as you're ready to come around, I'm going to bless you. But you've wasted twenty years."

You don't need to waste a minute. Financial freedom begins with recognizing the trust of ownership. Jay is a Jesus-follower from Ginghamsburg Church and a very successful business person. I study successful people. Rather than resent their success, I ask them what they're doing in order to learn from them. So we asked Jay and Lori what they are doing. They are a true demonstration of the devotion of rightful ownership.

(Jay) "My perception, even when I look back to childhood, is that I always liked money. When I got out of college and started my career and began seeing the possibilities of achieving the American dream, my focus was to become a millionaire as quickly as I could.

I was always a very controlling person—and I'm not just talking about things. Whether people, places, or things, I always wanted to be in control. And from a financial standpoint, I wanted to be a slumlord. I'd watch those get-rich-quick real estate programs late at night and started buying houses, fixing them up, and working two or three other jobs. It was a total focus on self and feeling good. Achieving financial dreams was a way to make me feel good. And then, when that wasn't happening or I was having to work far too much, then I started taking the edge off through alcohol and other chemicals. In my haste to attain the American dream, I lost my health and basically became spiritually, mentally, and physically bankrupt at the age of 28."

(Lori) "When we were in the pits, I was feeling very empty inside, thinking 'How did I find myself in the midst of this horrible, total mess?' I had a relationship with Christ at that point in time and I did pray with friends. We had a small group and we would meet every now and then. They knew some of the things that we were going through, and they would pray with me — and for us."

(Jay) "One night right before I was about to pass out in my chair, I finally put my arms up in the sky and I said, 'God help me. I don't care what it takes, help me.' The next day, Lori was a part of an intervention that ultimately got me into a treatment center. I can remember as clear as if it was yesterday. I was sitting in this treatment center in the lounge late at night by myself, and I was going through my mail. There was a little book that one of Lori's friends had sent me that contained instructions on how to turn your life over to Christ. In the past, I thought I was already "fixed"— I didn't need that. I was so bankrupt at this point in time that I read the book. I said, 'Alright, Christ. Obviously I can't do it; you can. It's time that I let you.' Lori and I had nothing. My profession is such that I couldn't afford to go back to work and didn't know if I was going to have a job. We had to sell our properties; I sold a huge part of my coin collection, which I had for years. And I look back on that, and this may sound a weird, but I'm glad it all happened, because I got rid of all the stuff that almost took me to my grave."

For me today, I gather strength in turning the ownership of everything I have over to God. And it starts with my family; I don't own my kids. I'm here to guide, lead, and help them grow. It's the same way with my marriage and my business."

(Lori) "There's more freedom in Christ and freedom when you give yourself over to Christ and realize that everything we have is not really ours at all."

(Jay) "It's been amazing what God's done to bless that business. We've actually grown exponentially from a financial standpoint and from how many people we get to provide care for—and also how many employees who experience a positive impact in their lives. It's been an unbelievable journey; something I know I could never do on my own. God's given me an opportunity to be a part of this as long as I give it to him."[1]

God is not a respecter of persons. God does not desire to bless Jay and Lori more than God seeks to bless you. Transformation begins with our willingness to release all that we are and have into the hands of God. Surrender. Financial freedom requires the true devotion of rightful ownership.

---

[1] View the Jay and Lori Meyer digital story on the DVD within *Money Matters: Financial Freedom for All God's Churches* (ISBN 0687495555). Or view it at www.ginghamsburg.org/mm.

It All Matters: **Further Steps For** **Freedom Finders**

1. **You already have "in your hand"** everything you need for financial freedom. Make a list of five assets, talents, traits, or experiences that could show financial value if given to God and used well.

2. **Think about what you've learned** in these first two chapters. How does your worldview need to be transformed to the worldview of Jesus?

   • I need to see God as rightful owner of my life and possessions.

   • I must deal with my debt, allowing me to be more present to the needs of others.

   • I must "release" something to God that feels difficult for me to let go.

"The jar of flour will not be used up and the jug of oil will not run dry..."

Surrender, Trust, and Freedom

Some time later the brook dried up because there had been no rain in the land. Then the word of the LORD came to Elijah: "Go at once to Zarephath of Sidon and stay there. I have commanded a widow in that place to supply you with food."

So he went to Zarephath. When he came to the town gate, a widow was there gathering sticks. He called to her and asked, "Would you bring me a little water in a jar so I may have a drink?" As she was going to get it, he called, "And bring me, please, a piece of bread."

"As surely as the LORD your God lives," she replied, "I don't have any bread—only a handful of flour in a jar and a little oil in a jug. I am gathering a few sticks to take home and make a meal for myself and my son, that we may eat it-and die."

Elijah said to her, "Don't be afraid. Go home and do as you have said. But first make a small cake of bread for me from what you have and bring it to me, and then make something for yourself and your son. For this is what the LORD, the God of Israel, says: 'The jar of flour will not be used up and the jug of oil will not run dry until the day the LORD gives rain on the land.'"— 1 Kings 17:7-14

In 1 Kings 17 we find the story of a man named Elijah, a prophet of God, who became God's means to respond to another person's need. Often I hear the question from unbelievers as well as Christians, "Why does God allow people to starve? Why does God allow all the suffering in the world?" God does not allow anyone to starve. You and I are the ones allowing the starvation because we do not understand God's perspective on money. God uses the resources of people. That's why it's so important that we are good stewards of the resources that God has entrusted to us. Those resources become the means to answer somebody else's need and somebody else's prayer. God releases heaven's resources to God's children through God's children.

God releases heaven's resources to God's children through God's children.

When considering God's provision, do you use the formula of human computation or the power of divine math? The biblical principles for financial freedom challenge us to live within our means. That's a given. There's always more to what God wants to do in us and through us, however. Remember what God said to Moses, *"What is that in your hand?"* Here's what Elijah says to this widow: *"Use what's in your hand."* God's word to us is to live out of what we have, out of the resources God provides.

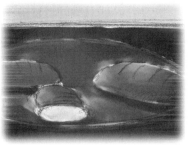

Our problem is that we doubt God and see only what we have. We factor human computation instead of divine math. And what do we see? "I only have a little. I don't really have anything, just this little bit." We habitually forget that a little in the hands of God is a lot.

Surrender What You Have

When we look at the miracles of Jesus we see that God never makes something from nothing. When five thousand people were hungry, Jesus didn't snap his fingers and have Big Macs fall out of the sky. It was the same when Jesus' friends needed wine at the wedding feast. Jesus didn't snap his fingers and make wine appear. He took what they had—water—and turned it into wine. Jesus appreciated the two pennies that the widow had to give. The miracle comes from what you have, not from what you don't have. In the same way, when we've got bills to pay we can't think that God's going to make money appear out of nothing and spontaneously pay off our bills. God always asks us to surrender and place in God's hands what we already have—and then we trust. Jesus takes a few fish and a few pieces of bread as if to say, Give it to me. You haven't done a good job with it. Give it to me. Surrender your finances to God, and watch what God will do. And remember that any time you use a charge card, you're using something you don't have. If you had it, you wouldn't have to charge it! God will only bless what you have.

God always asks us to surrender and place in God's hands what we already have—and then we trust.

Think of the incredible assets that God gives us in Christ Jesus. Many have received the gift of Jesus Christ and experienced eternal life as our own. We have the Holy Spirit and all of the assets of heaven, but God will not release those assets until we surrender to the Spirit that is in us. As long as we keep acting out of our wishes and our appetites and what we want to do with our money, God's not going to bless it. God's not going to release the resources of the Holy Spirit. But as we surrender to the Spirit that's in us, we are converted to the mind of Christ. Remember, there is one new birth but many conversions. There are areas of our life in which we've been "born again" but we've not been converted. We don't know the blessing of God until we're converted. When we are converted in our finances, we have the mind of Christ about our finances. What an incredible asset! With all of the creativity of Christ, think of the unlimited possibilities and potential.

Divine Math

When I was appointed to lead a congregation, I looked at the tiny church with human eyes, and I was tempted to do human computation instead of divine math. I saw a small, outdated church building in a terrible location, sixteen miles from a city with a population of only 180,000.

This rural church was three miles outside a town with a population of only 6,000. Human computation revealed no miracles in the future, and the financial resources were meager at best. The entire budget of the church was $27,000 per year, and everything came out of that modest amount: the children's educational resources, the utilities, my salary—everything we did. Carolyn and I drove the first car that ever came out of our New Path Car Ministry[2], just so we'd be able to stay out of debt. It was a 1966 Volkswagen with bright flames painted on the front.

We didn't look at our new venture through our own eyes, however. The whole Christian perspective is that we live with a resurrection worldview. Resurrections don't make sense. They're not rational. You can't explain what God did when he raised Jesus from the dead.

Discipline and Delayed Gratification

There are two life practices that are essential for living within your means: discipline and delayed gratification. First, God is concerned with creating in us a Christ-like character. You're going to die, and if you ascend the way you are, look out heaven! Right now God is developing the character of Christ in you. The character of Christ comes through discipline, not through credit. Discipline begins in your finances. If you're not disciplined in your finances, you cannot be disciplined in other areas of your life.

---

[2]The New Path Car Ministry is a program that accepts used cars and gives them to applicants in our region, who demonstrate a need for transportation.

If you're not disciplined in your finances, you cannot be disciplined in other areas of your life. The second life practice is delayed gratification. You live in a world that is instant. You are conditioned to think, "I want it right now." You are part of the generation that invented fast food. For example, I get frustrated when something doesn't come up right away on my new laptop. Yesterday a co-worker was helping me figure out how to use a program on it, and I said, "What is taking so long for this to come up? I thought this was supposed to be fast." He said, "It is fast." But it's not fast enough for me! Everything in our culture is about speed! Instant! Right now! But guess what? Character is not developed right now. Character is cultivated through delayed gratification.

Character is cultivated through delayed gratification.

One of the greatest frustrations I see in many people is college debt. I have been shocked in recent conversations with a number of young people. One recent graduate told me that he had $30,000 worth of college debt and $10,000 in credit card debt. It is common to have $30,000 to $90,000 of college debt, but this is not healthy. One of the best things parents can do for our children is to live with delayed gratification so our children do not have college debt. Most children have college debt because parents did not practice delayed gratification.

While growing up, every year we took a great vacation. My dad bought us whatever we wanted. He bought me the latest guitar amplifiers. And when it came time to go to college he said, "Sorry, son, we don't have it. You'll have to find a way to get there." I know no better reason to practice delayed gratification than to do everything you can to enable your children to get out of college debt-free. It's one of the best gifts you can give them, next to Jesus. Junior colleges can be a great option for the first couple years of college. It is also entirely possible to live at home and work while going to school. I had to live at home for my first three years of college and worked in a grocery store. I attended the two-year junior college, and then I completed the last two years at the University of Cincinnati.

By accepting the culture's expectation that our children should go into debt, so they can have "live away" college experiences, we condition them for decades to depend on credit rather than God's math. Don't get into the vicious cycle that begins with college debt.

Bigger Barns

Jesus also teaches us that too many possessions can be a liability. Freedom is the outcome of discipline. If we're not disciplined with little, we can't expect God to trust us with more. Consider how Jesus cautioned us in the Gospel of Luke.

> *Then he said to them, "Watch out! Be on your guard against all kinds of greed; a man's life does not consist in an abundance of his possessions." And he told them this parable: "The ground of a certain rich man yielded an abundant harvest. He thought to himself, 'What shall I do? I have no place to store my crops.' Then he said, 'This is what I'll do. I will tear down my barns and build bigger ones, and there I will store all my surplus grain. And I'll say to myself, 'You have plenty of grain laid up for many years. Take life easy; eat, drink and be merry.'" But God said to him, 'You fool! This very night your life will be demanded from you. Then who will get what you have prepared for yourself?' This is how it will be with anyone who stores up things for themselves but is not rich toward God.—Luke 12:14-21*

This particular rich man was really blessed; he had enough. Instead of realizing that he had enough, however, he continued building bigger and bigger warehouses.

Unfortunately, the more stuff you have, the more time and money it takes to take care of your stuff. Getting more stuff doesn't free you; it can make you into a slave. Galatians 5:1a reminds us that, *"It is for freedom that Christ has set us free."* Christ died for freedom. Christ set you free not to be a slave to anything else ever again. Because taking care of your stuff forces you to work more, you're not practicing Sabbath rhythms or relationships.

Getting more stuff doesn't free you; it can make you into a slave.

As a pastor I am often present with a person when he or she is dying. In the presence of death, not one person has ever said to me, "I wish I had had more stuff,"or, "I wish I'd made more money." I have not heard anyone say that in thirty-two years of being a pastor. Instead, I hear a person say, "I wish I would have spent more time with my kids." I hear that again and again and again. "I wish I would have spent more time serving." "I wish I would have spent more time helping people."

The Bible talks about hoarding as well. *"Stand firm, then"* we're warned, *and do not let yourselves be burdened again by a yoke of slavery"* (Galatians 5:1b). It's wise to know when you have enough and when you need to release the excess to other people. God provided for the Israelites every day when they were out in the desert wilderness. He said, *"I will rain manna from heaven."* People were gathering every day just what they needed. But some people didn't trust that God would provide tomorrow, and they gathered more than they needed. It became full of maggots and smelled. Excesses that we accumulate will eventually become full of maggots and stink. The key to living within your means is to trust God's promise of provision. First Kings 17:14 sums this up, *"For this is what the Lord, the God of Israel, says...."* It's all based on what God says. It's all based on what God promises. Everything God says comes to pass. The Bible says every promise in Jesus is "Yes." *"For no matter how many promises God has made, they are 'Yes' in Christ"* (2 Corinthians 1:20).

Building a Trust

> *For this is what the Lord, the God of Israel, says: "The jar of flour will not be used up and the jug of oil will not run dry until the day the Lord sends rain on the land."*—1 Kings 17:14

The key word in establishing financial health and freedom is the word *trust*.

Those who work with financial investments understand about building a trust. The concept of a trust refers to building trust with God, setting up a trust with God. In the story from 1 Kings we see that fear is creating the woman's impoverished thinking, and fear is the opposite of trust. When you're afraid that you don't have enough, however, it's because you're doing human computation rather than divine math. You are looking through your human eyes. Remember, the radical conversion in Christianity is that we no longer live by what we see; we live with a resurrection worldview. Resurrections don't make sense. So we walk by faith, not by sight.

Remember, the radical conversion in Christianity is that we no longer live by what we see; we live with a resurrection worldview. Resurrections don't make sense.

True faith involves three things: your head, your heart, and your hand. It does not become resource-releasing faith from God's perspective until it involves all three.

A Head-full of Promises

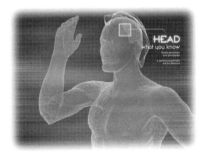

First of all, you must know the promises and principles of God. People of resource-releasing faith come to the word of God with open hearts and open notebooks. You know that if God is speaking to you through the Scripture, and you act on it, it's going to be released into your life. When you spend time with God and in the Scripture each day, it's not just for a little religious exercise. No, it is so you can know the truth of God and then practice the truth of God. You can't practice it if you don't know it.

That's also why I don't care how boring the speaker is when I am traveling somewhere. I always have a pencil and a piece of paper. If Jesus' name is mentioned, the Holy Spirit is going to speak. I know that when I don't do what God is asking of me, I am missing the mark, and that is called sin. What we are doing with our money is a result of obedience or sin. There are no gray areas between obedience and sin.

Head to Heart

Through Isaiah 58 we know that God's priority is the poor. Our generosity is expected to flow toward poor people. I have a bracelet on my arm, and it says "Sudan." Every time I look at it, it reminds me of my spending habits and my holiday budget. This bracelet reminds me that my family is preparing for a simple Christmas and we'll bring a miracle offering to the

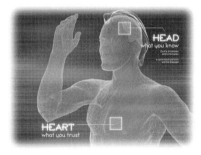

church, because I know what God's priority is. You have power with God by your actions toward people. (Visit The Sudan Project site at www.ginghamsburg.org/sudan.)

Once you know the truth of God, you must transfer it to your heart. I've heard the greatest distance in the world is the distance from your head to your heart. You have God's truth in your heart when you go beyond knowing it, to trusting it.

How can you tell that you trust God's truth? When I was a kid, my dad taught me to love baseball. I grew up in Cincinnati. The Cincinnati Reds and Crosley Field were historic. I'd say, "Dad, can you get us some tickets?" And he'd say, "Okay, I'll get us some tickets for next Thursday." On Thursday we'd board the city bus and ride to Crosley Field. I didn't have to ask again, never had to ask, "Dad, are we still going to the game?" Once my dad said it, I had it. And in the very same way every promise in Jesus is "yes" to you. That's moving it from the head to the heart. You can tell when it's hit your heart because it truly becomes faith and is released through your hand. It is because of God's promised provision that I can give to God's purpose.

Heart to Hand

In 1 Kings 17:15 we see that *"She (the widow) went away and did as Elijah had told her."* She did it. *"So there was food every day for Elijah and for the woman and her family."* Notice the order and the priority; notice to whom she released it. You must release it before God can increase it. She used it for God's purpose. She proved trustworthy of God's trust. So

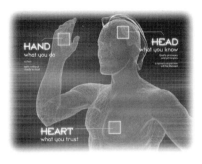

the jar never ran empty for her and her son. In 1 Kings 17:16, every word that God speaks comes to pass: *"For the jar of flour was not used up and the jug of oil did not run dry, in keeping with the word of the LORD spoken by Elijah."* There is a cause and effect relationship between generosity and increase in your life.

Second Corinthians 9:11a says, *"You will be made rich in every way so that you can be generous on every occasion."* God's purpose in creating wealth is so you can be generous. What is God's economy? God answers people's prayer through us. God has never caused one person on this earth to starve; it's our hardness of heart that kills people. On judgment day we're going to see that the things we blamed on God were actually our doing. God provides for our needs so we can be generous toward the needs of others.

Malachi 3:10 calls us to, *"Bring the whole tithe into the storehouse that there may be food in my house."* A tithe is the first ten percent. "Food in his house" doesn't mean a roof on a church. It is rather God's economy to meet the needs in the world. *"'Test me in this,' says the LORD Almighty, 'and see if I will not throw open the floodgates of heaven and pour out so much blessing that you will not have room enough for it.'"* There's a cause and effect relationship between generosity and increase. God is saying to his children, *"Test me."* We must test God. If all you do is believe it in your head without trusting it in your heart and releasing it with your hand, you've never tested God. You've never experienced the blessing of God's promise.

Whatever It Takes

Are you willing to do what it takes to get well and be free? God is not going to snap some fingers and put your financial picture together. This book was not written merely so you could know some things about improving wealth and managing finances. These insights are offered to help you see that God's blessing is poised to flow through your life toward others.

You may have begun practicing these principles at some point in your life, and because of a lack of discipline, or due to a series of difficulties, such as declining health or broken relationships, the practices all went to hell again. "Hell" in this context is the absence of the presence of God. Perhaps you are living out of hell in your finances. It's time for God to redeem your situation and take you to a new place. Check out this story of a young couple, Lance and Amber Salyers, who decided to get well several years ago as they listened to God's word for financial freedom:

(Lance) "Amber and I met in college and got married, and right away we started to live off credit cards. Debt just started to build. We didn't have any sense of a budget. We had no idea of where our money was going. And so by the time we graduated from college, the debt was getting bigger and bigger. The more we would try to say, 'Well we're just going to spend less,' nothing would happen because we didn't have a plan.

After three years of law school we moved here. Just our credit card debt, not our student loans, was at $20,000. The only thing we really had to show for it by the time we got to Ohio was a washer and dryer, and our bed, and that was it. Everything else was just gone. In college, we spent it on eating or going to the movies or buying gifts for other people at Christmas when we should have said, "No, we don't have the money and that's not what it's about." We were working to pay off stuff we didn't even have anymore.

Once we got to our church, we heard a series of messages about stewardship and signed up for the "Will You Grow?" commitment campaign. But then we faced a dilemma, which was: How much do we give versus how much do we use to get out of debt? We prayed about it, and talked about it, and finally came to the conclusion that we're going to give as if we don't have the debt and we will work our debt reduction around our giving. So we started giving ten percent. We thought that was what we should do.

We sat down and had a serious "budget" meeting. We met in the office for three hours and just hashed out, "Okay, how are we going to do this?" For each month we can set "X amount of dollars" aside for this and "X amount of dollars" aside for that. For eating out, it was $30 a month. We'd go out to eat once. We loved, after church, going out to eat with friends. Once a month we can do that. The other three or four weeks, it's "sorry we have to go home." Our food budget is out. And so we'd have to go home. For us personally, whether it's to get some clothes or what-ever—it was ten bucks a month. If you wanted something that was $50, you were going to have to wait five months. It was brutally hard. That's just how it had to be.

The numbers don't add up. There's no other explanation for us, other than it was God taking care of us because we were now walking in the road that God wanted us to walk. We had the resources to give. We had the resources to get out of debt, and we didn't go without what we needed.

Neither one of us got any raises. Amber works as a teacher and I work for the county. As lawyers go, I don't make a third of what I could make at a private firm if I had gone that route. But somehow those loaves and fishes multiplied to where the debt is dead and we gave more than we thought we ever could have given.

Amber's car is now paid for. It's phenomenal. It's an extra bunch of money each month that we didn't have yesterday.

Amber and I have been married about nine and a half years; we're now expecting our first child in a couple months. When that baby comes, we're not going to still be sending most of our money each month to pay for movies we went to in college. We can use that money to provide for our child. And instead of looking backward all the time each month, our finances and our lives can be looking forward to whatever God has in store for us."[3]

---

[3] View Lance and Amber's story, "Freedom" on the DVD that is packaged with *Money Matters: Financial Freedom For All God's Churches*, or go to www.ginghamsburg.org/mm.

Freedom Finders

Further Steps For

It All Matters:

1. All of God's promises are "yes" in Jesus. As you embark on your journey towards financial freedom, choose one Scripture verse that will be your promise as you move forward through good times and seasons of challenge.

2. Are you ready to "test" God towards financial freedom? If so, there are several steps you must take in order to discover God's transforming freedom in your finances:

   a. Sit down and make a plan to get out of debt right now. Debt is not the will of God for your life.

   b. Establish and live within a budget. Jesus isn't going to snap his fingers and make your money work. If you want to do what it takes to get well, you must establish a budget and live within that budget. Seek the help and accountability of a financially free friend or counselor if needed.

   c. Commit to regular giving. There's a cause and effect relationship between generosity and increase. Some people say, "Well, I'm going to get out of debt and then give." God's not going to bless you until God can trust you and see that you're using it for other people.

In the next part of the book we'll take a look at that debt and equip you to begin your first steps toward financial freedom.

Part Two

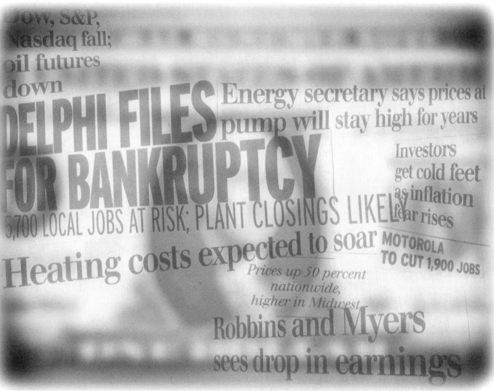

The Commitment to Debt-Free Living

Stewardship 101

*"For where your treasure is, there your heart will be also."—
Jesus, Matthew 6:21*

The purpose of Jesus' work in our lives is to set us free in every dimension. Our spending habits are one of the major dimensions that affect our spiritual and financial health. It is very difficult in our culture to experience the kind of financial freedom that Jesus offers. Through various forms of media, marketing directors call to us from every direction. We're bombarded the moment we turn on our TVs, radios, and log into our computers each morning. Mail-order catalogs, displaying everything we never knew we needed, pour into our homes, especially during the Christmas season. Pleas for our money spiral completely out of control, taunting our sensibilities with everything from coats to cashews.

Foolish Decisions

One of the catalogs I've received for several years is called "Territory Ahead." Several years ago I spotted the advertisement for a 100% cotton canvas bag for $159.00... a *cotton* bag! Now what fool would buy that? I don't know why I did it. One day I noticed that bag lying in the corner of my office, where it's been ever since I bought it. I was stunned when I checked the catalog to see how much I'd paid for it. I can now see that it's not really a practical piece of luggage. It doesn't protect my computer. It doesn't have dividers or special compartments, and it isn't the right shape to be a briefcase.

Because of its pricey tag I tried to force myself to use it as an overnight bag. On one occasion I tried packing it for an out of town conference, thinking that all I'd need would be a Dobbs kit, a change of underwear, pants, and a shirt. It didn't take me long to realize that the pants and shirt would become wrinkled disasters by the next day, so I still haven't used the bag. Apparently, I paid for an illustration—$160 for an illustration.

How many things like that bag do you have sitting around your house, for which you've piddled away good money? It worries me to think of how many unwanted possessions I've acquired. These impulses remind me that financial health and freedom is a result of aligning our spending habits with the values of God, and every financial decision is in reality a spiritual decision.

The effectiveness of your life is not found in what you own, but in the stewardship of what you've been given.

The effectiveness of your life is not found in what you own, but in the stewardship of what you've been given. You have everything you need to start right now fulfilling God's purpose in your life and to ultimately achieve financial health.

In 1 Samuel 17:38-40, David demonstrates an insightful example of this promise.

> *Saul dressed David in his own (Saul's) tunic. He put a coat of armor on him and a bronze helmet on his head. David fastened on his sword over the tunic and tried walking around, because he was not used to them.*
>
> *"I cannot go in these," David said to Saul, "because I am not used to them." So he took them off. Then he took his staff in his hand, chose five smooth stones from the stream, put them in the pouch of his shepherd's bag and, with his sling in his hand, approached the Philistine.*

David was going against a giant named Goliath, and David was but a young teenager, not even fully grown. Initially this overwhelming endeavor tempted David to use Saul's resources. He was a kid trying to walk in a grown man's armor— but he couldn't even move in it. He told Saul that he couldn't function well  because he was not used to that awkward uniform. David ended up taking the armor off, picking up his staff, five stones from the stream, and the sling he'd used to defend many a helpless lamb. David was a shepherd, and with that simple but familiar instrument of his trade he approached the Philistine.

Like David, you already have what you need. You can't wear another person's clothes, even if those possessions promise security and significance. You must identify and put to use the resources God has already placed in *your* hand. And if you're faithful and obedient with what God has given you, God will multiply it for God's purpose.

Dealing with Debt

We must think of ourselves as God's investment partners rather than people of need.

To be faithful and obedient with what God's given you, you must deal with your debt. Debt is not God's will for your life.

The Bible says we should never be the borrower but we should always be the lender. In other words, we must think of ourselves as God's investment partners rather people of need. Proverbs 22:7 tells us why: *"The rich rule the poor, and the borrower is slave to the lender."* Jesus died to set you free, but as long as you owe even a dollar to someone, you will always be a slave to that person.

Consider a practical example of why the borrower is always slave to the lender. Let's say you owe $5,560 on your credit card. That is equivalent to one trip for a family of four to Disney World, plus a three-day cruise. Despite opening offers of 7.5 percent upon accepting a credit card, the interest on a typical credit card is 18 percent. (The contributors to political campaigns are credit card companies, and the laws work in their favor.)

Let's say you are late in making a payment. Read the fine print on your credit cards. With many of your credit cards, your rate goes to 23.4 percent when you are late in paying. If you're late on a payment, the average late fee you pay is twenty-nine dollars, plus your interest rate will increase. Your credit card company has a guaranteed rate of return: 18 percent of what you continue to owe. (Please note that no one gets a guaranteed rate of return except these companies.) You pay $1,000 a year in interest on the amount that has a minimum payment of $80 a month. Most people pay only the minimum payment; so at the end of 40 years you still owe the initial amount. You took a trip to Disneyland or Disney World 40 years ago, and you still haven't paid for it. You have merely paid $1,000 a year interest to the shareholders in the credit card company. Your credit card company during that 40 years charged compounded interest at 18 percent and made over $40,000 from your $5,560 investment. Do you see why they want to keep you on the line? Can you understand why they keep calling you and offering you more credit, in some cases 2 or 3 times a week?

If you took that same $1,000 a year you pay in interest to the credit card **Remember, getting out of debt is hard work. It is a commitment. It begins with plastic surgery, cutting up those credit cards, which is an act of faith.** company and invested it at twelve percent (which over the long term of 40 years is an honest return), you would have earned $952,193 (tax deferred), just by putting in $1,000 every year. You say you don't have $1,000? Yes, you do! You're giving it to the credit card company every year. This is why the borrower is always a slave to the lender, and if you're going to be obedient and faithful with what you have in your hand, you first and foremost have to deal with debt.

Remember, getting out of debt is hard work. It is a commitment. It begins with plastic surgery, cutting up those credit cards, which is an act of faith.

In faith we depend on God instead of Visa or MasterCard for our needs. See the difference?

Getting out of debt is not only hard work; it is very humbling as well. Check out a few examples of people in one church family and their plans for getting out of debt:

(Michele) "I made the decision to move in with my parents. They made the offer, and I was not totally excited about it at age thirty. But I knew it would allow me to get rid of the debt that I had accumulated, and in the last year I have been able to knock out all of my credit card debt."

(Francis) "I have a set of V-drums that I bought about two years ago, and I love those things. You can make all kinds of sounds, any kind of sound that you want, and I could play in the basement for hours and nobody knew I was there. But I plan to sell the V-drums to put the money toward credit card debt and home equity debt. It's more important for us to get out of debt than it is to be able to sit there with these V-drums that look good and sound good."

(Erica) "One way is I've taken on a small extra job to help pay down some of the debt. Another way is we are selling some things that we don't necessarily need or use very often. My husband bought a hunting bow a couple years ago, and I think he used it once and not even really in the way it was supposed to be used, so we're getting rid of that. We are also getting rid of a waterbed that we no longer use."

(Dwayne) "My parents travel most of the year—they are snowbirds—so since they're gone most of the time, I was able to move back into their house and alleviate the rent payment. I am also putting my motorcycle up for sale, which is a hard thing to do, but it's something I need to do to pay off some of that high-interest debt."

(Sherri) "I sought out a cheaper apartment so my rent would be less, took on a second job to supplement my income, gave up things like cable TV and extra expenses and really shifted my thinking toward a focus of getting out of debt."[4]

Debt affects every area of your life. Fifty-six percent of divorces are tied to financial tension. As we look at financial health, this is really when we must trust God for the healing God wants to do, and we must be absolutely sure we want to be healed. Remember the physically challenged man whom Jesus

---

[4] You can also view these segments entitled "How Are You Getting Out of Debt?" on the DVD within *Money Matters: Financial Freedom For All God's Churches,* or view it at www.ginghamsburg.org/mm.

Do you really want to get well? encountered in John 5:6? *"When Jesus saw him lying there and learned that he had been in this condition for a long time, he asked him, 'Do you want to get well?'"* Jesus asked that question to the one person who requested physical healing: *"Do you want to get well?"* And that's the question the Lord asks you now as you consider your financial brokenness. Do you really want to get well?

Release What Is In Your Hand

The LORD said, "Throw it on the ground." Moses threw it on the ground and it became a snake, and he ran from it (Exodus 4:3).

The church is filled with people who believe in the purpose of God, but have yet to actively yield to the purpose of God. When you realize that you have everything in your hand that you need for God's purpose and your financial health, God asks you to do something more. You must go beyond believing in God's purpose to releasing it to God's purpose. The church is filled with people who believe in the purpose of God, but have yet to actively yield to the purpose of God. You will not experience the miracle of what God can do until you yield, releasing all you possess.

How much must you yield? Ten percent? No, the earth and all it contains belong to the Lord. You must yield 100 percent of your resources and energies to God and God's purpose. God owns your passion, God owns your vision, and God owns your success. God owns the increase in your life.

The earth is the Lord's, and everything in it.

psalm 24:1

In stark contrast to the power of our Creator God is the undermining work of Evil. Evil has an agenda of financial brokenness and paralysis, and Evil tempts us towards sin in all of our money matters. Put bluntly, sin is present whenever we worship the creature rather than the Creator. Sin is present whenever we work for self rather than for God. When we release what God has given us, however, our job, experiences, talents, and resources become our acts of worship. When we release, we truly begin to worship God and not ourselves. We truly begin to work for the Creator instead of working for ourselves. Recognizing God's ownership and releasing ourselves to it is the critical first step in financial freedom. It is an amazingly practical process that involves establishing and living by a budget. It doesn't matter how little you make or how much you make, when you establish and live by a budget you're living within the boundaries of what you already have.

Discipline and Christ-like Character

God's purpose in your life is to build in you Christ-like character, and this life on earth is for the purpose of training and character development. You **You are being prepared for** are being prepared for eternity, and God **eternity, and God is currently** is currently building that enduring Christ-**building that enduring** like character in you. Christ-like **Christ-like character in you.** character comes through discipline, and discipline begins in the area of our finances and possessions. That's why Jesus said, *"For where your treasure is, there your heart will be also"* (Matthew 6:21).

This is one area of discipline that Carolyn and I have accomplished in our 32 years of marriage. I still mess up once in a while and leak away money that could be used in other places, but we have successfully lived by what we call an "envelope system." In the first envelope we put the tithe. That is the 10 percent of the gross income we make. In May 1976, I made a commitment to the Lord that the first 10 percent of everything I made would go to the Lord. Next we put our house payment in an envelope, then our utility payment, then our grocery payment in an envelope. We have an envelope for gifts—Christmas, birthdays, graduations—twelve months of gifts. Now when Christmas comes, plastic is not an option. We can only spend what's in the envelope. We've come to birthdays when there has been only fourteen dollars in the envelope, so what do we do? We get extremely creative, because we can only use what's in our hand. From newspapers to insurance, everything we spend in a year is divided out by twelve months. We can't spend what's not in an envelope. This system works very well for us.

Monday is my day off. So we went to a movie, and at the end of the film I said, "Let's go out to dinner." Carolyn said, "There's only four dollars left in the envelope." We went home. I could have said, "Wednesday I'm speaking at such and such and I'll be making some extra money, so it won't hurt if we go to dinner." But we don't do that. It wasn't in our envelope, so we came home and made spaghetti. Others, I've discovered, have a more virtual envelope system by using a computer program and recording each expenditure as it arises. (Online banking software also records your transactions, but it may not create any more discipline than a credit card statement.) The important step is to have some sort of effective plan! It doesn't matter how much or how little we have, it's living within the means

It doesn't matter how much or how little we have, it's living within the means of what we have.

of what we have. Plenty of persons who make more than $100,000 per year have the same difficulty with discipline as a person making $25,000. God is building in us Christ-like character, and Christ-like character comes through discipline. We use what God has put in our hand.

One budget formula works very well when you're getting started on a budget. It is simply 10-10-80.The first 10 percent of what you make goes to God. The next 10 percent goes into investing for your promising future. Every farmer knows you don't eat all your seed. You put aside seed corn to plant next year. So always pay yourself after you pay God, and then live off the remaining 80 percent. As you grow in discipline these first two categories increase: the ability to give more than 10 percent to the Lord and to save more than 10 percent. What kind of promising future do I want to have? That's how much seed I am I putting out there. And we don't live off of the whole eighty percent, because we want to be free to have the opportunity to bless other people as needs arise.

I'll advise you the same way I've advised my own children: Don't go out and choose a job based on money; rather, get in touch with your passion. Your passion belongs to God. Pour yourself into your passion and trust God's

Your passion belongs to God. Pour yourself into your passion and trust God's provision.

provision. In my life, God has blessed our family with education for our children, and the money to pay for it. I could never have paid for their college if God hadn't provided resources outside of my job, the outlet for my passion. I've poured myself into that passion, and God's anointed it. I never sought the money; I simply pursued my passion and trusted God for my provision.

Pursuing Your Passion in Work

Carolyn and I are both so busy that we have no time to iron our clothing. Sometimes we're running down to the basement to iron a shirt ten minutes before I must be somewhere. I went to a meeting at the church and was talking with someone who is part of the church. I asked what she did for a living, and she answered that she and her husband are on disability. I said, "Well, how do you eat?" She said, "Well, I like to clean houses and iron." I said, "You like to clean houses and you like to IRON?" "Oh yeah, I'm good at it," she replied. I said, "You know when I take my shirts to the dry cleaners, I must re-iron them many times because they screw it up. How much do you charge?" She said, "One dollar each piece, and I pick up and deliver!" So the next day she had 27 pieces from the Slaughters! And they were back that day at five o'clock. This is the kind of provision that we see when we pour ourselves into our passion and trust God's provision.

Trustworthy Servants

Then the LORD said to him, "Reach out your hand and take it by the tail." So Moses reached out and took hold of the snake and it turned back into a staff in his hand (Exodus 4:4). God trusts you as well. When you give it all up, God trusts you to pick it back up, but it won't be the same staff that you had in your hand the first time! You now hold something in your hand that is the very resource of God. He said, *Pick that thing up by the tail*, and what you've got by the tail is the resource of heaven.

You now hold something in your hand that is the very resource of God.

Moses had a conversion in his thinking. When he began, he was asked what he had in his hand, and he said, *"I've got a stick."* But by verse twenty he saw that his talents, his skills, his gifts, and his resources were not his own. He released them to God and when he picked the snake tail back up, it became the staff of God. From that point on Moses was a changed man. Armed with these resources he was able to part the sea and call water from a rock. There was a huge conversion in Moses' life as there can be in your own. Conversion is when you change from your thinking and practice about finances to God's thinking and practice.

Conversion is when you change from your thinking and practice about finances to God's thinking and practice.

Success whispers, "I want to make more money"… "I want to live in a nicer house"… "I want to be able to retire at a certain age and live the kind of lifestyle I want" … "I want, I want… " The focus is always on me. God cannot use that kind of attitude. Significance, on the other hand, is when the focus is not on "I" but the focus is on "God," what God wants to do through you to bless and refresh other people. Moses used that stick from that day forward to bless, refresh, and deliver people. Jesus referred to this attitude as building treasures in heaven. The effectiveness of life is not about ownership but stewardship—managing what God has given you for the purpose of blessing and refreshing other people.

The effectiveness of life is not about ownership but stewardship—managing what God has given you for the purpose of blessing and refreshing other people.

God has created this change in my life—from self-centered materialism to

Jesus' sacrificial worldview—and now I ask myself, "What was I thinking?" Do you ever look at a new possession and wonder, "What was I thinking?" The priority of God must become our priority in every area of life. Proverbs 22:9 asserts that *"The generous will themselves be blessed, for they share* **The priority of God** *their food with the poor."* God is going to bless **must become our prior-** generous people who share God's priority and **ity in every area of life.** desire to provide for all of God's children.

Bottom line, God is looking for people to trust. Trust begins with getting rid of your debt and then picking up what God has given you and using it to bless God and refresh other people. Are you a trustworthy servant?

Further Steps For Freedom Finders

It All Matters:

1. **Confession is good for the soul.** What are some of the foolish decisions you have made in the past concerning financial purchases? What new decisions are you making that will prevent you from repeating this mistake?

2. **We must think of ourselves as God's investment partners rather than people of need.** In what way have you depended on credit (or the generosity of other people) that now must change, so that you can become God's investment partner?

3. **God's priorities must become our priorities.** In order to move from self-centered materialism to Jesus' sacrificial worldview, we must take intentional steps. Consider serving the less fortunate in some way during this journey toward financial freedom.

"Let no debt remain outstanding..."

Chapter Five

Steps to Debt-free Living

Let no debt remain outstanding, except the continuing debt to love one another, for whoever loves others has fulfilled the law.—Romans 13:8

The first priority we must address in the quest for financial freedom is to eliminate all debt. You must grasp this before you attempt anything further. God's law says to "*Owe no one anything except to love one another*" (NRSV). Now that's the word of God.

Faith is future focused, and debt ties our future to the past.

As long as we continue going into debt, even though we're under the protection of grace through Jesus Christ, we're going to be poor; we're never going to know financial freedom. Faith is future focused, and debt ties our future to the past. Here is the story of David, and his climb out of the poverty of debt:

(David) For as long as I can remember, I wanted to be a millionaire. In fact when I was fourteen, I started answering ads in magazines on how to become a millionaire. At first I wanted to be a millionaire by twenty-one, then it was twenty-five, then thirty…and it just never happened. I wasted a lot of money and accumulated a lot of credit card debt through some bad investments and trying to become rich. I was an expert on rolling over money; I was cash advancing credit cards to pay other credit card payments. It got to a point where I could only meet minimum amounts. I had between ten and twelve credit cards that had significant balances.

Filing bankruptcy wiped out my debt, but it didn't change my financial spending habits at all. I ended up getting divorced, losing my house, and moving into an apartment. Then I couldn't even afford that. I moved into a friend's basement, and I continued with the poor financial decisions. Once again I got myself into $50,000 of credit card debt. It wasn't like I didn't know how to handle money. I knew the practices in my mind, but in my heart I wasn't following them.

The plan I came up with three years ago was to commit to God, give to him everything I could as I pay off all of our debt, including our mortgage, within the next ten years. We have set up a budget and we're actually tracking every dime we spend now. We put aside for long-term savings; we save for vacation, Christmas, and there's money that goes into every one of those categories. In fact, I've kept my car now for seven years where in the past I would've gone out three years ago and bought a new car.

Once I committed to giving to God, in the last three years my income has increased twenty-five percent and I've been able to cut my debt in half. I have more money now and more to show for it than I ever did when I was living on credit card debt. So when you commit to being financially responsible, that doesn't mean you give up your life. That just means you're smart about how you spend your money."[5]

College students are especially vulnerable to credit card debt. Upon their graduation from high school they become inundated with credit card offers, and it is extremely easy to actually acquire a credit card. Entire campus events are staged with areas set up to award free T-shirts, hats, or Frisbees if you take the credit card. Here is the reason for why the credit card companies do this: In Chapter 4 you learned that a credit card company wants you to maintain a balance of at least $5500 (it's easy to keep that kind of a balance on a credit card). If they can get you, at age 18 or 19, to keep a balance of that much money for 40 years at eighteen percent interest, you'll give them $1,000 a year in interest. As a credit card company with the current corporate tax breaks, if they invest that money you give them ($40,000 over 40 years, just in interest) at 18 percent, they will make $4,163,213 from your money alone. Now why are creditors giving you free T-shirts and Frisbees? Forty years later you still owe five thousand and some dollars (many times over), you don't even remember what you've spent it on, and it's absolutely gone. If you begin with $1,000 and invest $1,000 per year at twelve percent interest (which, based on historical precedent, you can average over 40 years), you will have made $952,193 (if tax deferred).[6] Your $1000 investment is less than $100 a month. And what could happen if you save $2,000?[7]

Debt mortgages our future to the past, but there is good news: we don't have to stay there. Jesus came to liberate us. The very first step toward financial freedom is to stay out of debt. Either you're going to make someone else wealthy or, because you obey the law of God, God is going to entrust you with more, and your talents are going to multiply. Debt mortgages our future to the past, but there is good news: we don't have to stay there. Jesus came liberate us. Faith in God requires obedient action. When you're willing to obey and pay the cost with your best, God meets you with God's best.

[5] View David's story "I Wanna Be Rich" on the DVD within *Money Matters: Financial Freedom For All God's* Churches, or view it at www.ginghamsburg.org/mm.

[6] Even if your investment of $1,000 per year averages 8 percent over 40 years, you will have made $301,506 (if tax deferred):

[7] $1,904,387 at 12 percent annual return; $603,011 at 8 percent annual return (if tax deferred).

Faith in God requires obedient action. It's not enough to simply see our need to change or to deeply desire to handle our finances God's way. As in all areas of true life-transformation we must take intentional steps to find true liberation. *"No discipline seems pleasant at the time, but painful. Later on, however, it produces a harvest of righteousness and peace for those who have been trained by it"* (Hebrews 12:11). In the remaining part of this chapter, I will outline six steps for getting out of debt. Faithfulness to follow through with an intentional plan will pave the way for God to work powerfully. When you're willing to obey and pay the cost with your best, God meets you with his best.

Freedom Finders

Further Steps For

It All Matters:

1. **Pray.** Instead of trusting our own thoughts and energy, prayer appeals to our powerful parent who has promised to provide. We are making ourselves dependent upon God. Here is a suggested prayer you can use:

Gracious God, thank You for Your love and that You came to free me from all that enslaves me. I open my heart to You, and renew my desire to have You come into every area of my life. I thank You for what You are doing right now, Lord, in giving me new life and salvation. I want to surrender myself to You and confess my unwise habits that have kept us apart. Lord, I again submit myself to Your word. Your word says that Your people perish for lack of knowledge, and so I submit myself to Your word and make a commitment to do what I have to do to get out of debt. Give me strength; I'll do it in Your love. In the name of Jesus, Amen.

2. **List all of your debt.** Most people are unaware of the total sum of their debt. Debt includes car, house, and multiple credit cards. The average person has eight credit cards with outstanding balances. Most people never list exactly what is owed on each of those credit cards, but doing so is an essential step toward getting out of debt for good.

3. **Establish a written budget.** You can't spend what you don't make and what you don't have. With a budget, you are making a commitment to

spend less than what you make. You must create more than you consume, or you'll cease to exist.

Here's what's going to happen. You'll say it adds up, but it just doesn't add up. Because poor people think in terms of monthly payments, they don't think in terms of the big picture. They'll say, it doesn't add up. exactly!

So now you're going to have to think about what can be sold or downsized. Some of the wealthiest people at my church drive three- or four-year-old cars that they purchase from Avis for $5,000 or $6,000.

I know the regional vice-president of a major broadcast network, who is a Christian. During a trip to California, this friend picked Carolyn and me up at our hotel, to take us to his office. Before he arrived, I wondered out loud, "Can you imagine? I wonder what kind of car he's going to pick us up in? You know he's got the #1 parking spot at his office plaza!"

That vice-president picked us up in an '87 Cougar. We got into the car, and I asked, "What is this '87 Cougar bit?" In the parking lot we passed subordinates who drive Porsches and Mercedes. He said, "The person is a fool who puts his money in that which depreciates."

The car I own has over 110,000 miles on it, but I don't owe a thing on it. Now in my heart, I want that Infinity F-35. My toy list is huge, but staying out of the candy store is an essential discipline when budgeting toward financial freedom.

Your attitude toward budgeting will determine your success at getting out of debt. What can you eliminate for one year? Can you eliminate cable TV, cell phones, or high speed Internet? Start listing the things you could eliminate for one year. Your attitude toward budgeting will determine your success at getting out of debt.

While New Year's Day is a great time to start a new budget, I prefer to preach on Money Matters in the fall. In recent years I've preached that we need to simplify the "hell" out of Christmas. Jesus came to deliver us from evil. We've taught our grown children to live debt-free, and I find it greatly meaningful at Christmas when my daughter simply frames a neat picture of her and her husband, or she bakes something and puts it in a nice tin. It means so much to me when they put some energy into it instead of going out and buying a $50 sweater. I don't need another sweater!

4. Establish a repayment schedule. Most people stay in trouble because they can't see light at the end of the tunnel. Let's say you try to go on a diet and you're frustrated and you're not losing any weight, so . . . you eat. It's the same thing with debt. You can't see ever getting out of it, so you keep living the same way.

A debt repayment schedule requires an intentional plan. Let's say you have a $30,000 credit card debt. This may sound like a lot, but sadly many people in their mid-twenties are coming out of college with $90,000 of college debt and $30,000 in credit card debt. If you owe $30,000 in credit card debt, then you need a long-term plan to get out of debt, realizing that the first year you'll be able to pay down a portion, next year you'll be able to pay down an additional portion, perhaps taking up to ten years to pay off $30,000. You might have a three-year plan, a five-year plan, a seven-year plan, or a ten-year plan, but creating and maintaining that plan promises light at the end of the tunnel. Send your creditors a copy of your plan, and most creditors will back off. They want their money, and you've got a plan. They don't really want you to declare bankruptcy, and your plan shows them good faith. Believers should show good faith and do everything possible to avoid declaring bankruptcy.

Paying off smaller debts yields a greater sense of accomplishment, so start with the smaller debts. Build on that momentum and rather than say, "Oh, I've got extra money," take the extra money and flip it over to begin paying off the next smallest debt.

5. Consider ways of earning additional income. When attempting to generate extra income, too many people think, "Okay, I'm going to get another job at McDonalds," but $6 or $7 an hour may not bring the most effective results. Consider that there may be better ways to create additional income. I know a stay-at-home mom who has entered into an agreement with a restaurant to bake all their pies; she's doing a lot better than $6 an hour. On the other hand, I don't know how to do any-thing in my home, and it saves me more money to hire it done than to do it myself, especially if I buy an expensive tool that gets used once or twice. If I cut down a tree in the backyard, chances are it would fall down onto the fence, and I would wind up having to replace the fence!

Other people do possess these skills, however, so I can pay someone else who knows what he or she is doing to come over to my house and do it right.

Consider the skills you have that may be in some way marketable. Any number of possibilities can be nurtured within your talents. I've met people who, because they are computer-savvy, are building websites for organizations or small businesses. Because of my educational background, a production company in Hollywood paid me $300 to read a script and comment on it when the movie was in pre-production. It required two evenings of work. That's pretty good! I know moms who have a daycare in their own home. They are trained to watch two or three additional children and effectively add additional income without needing to pay for childcare themselves. Think of ways you can create additional income.

6. Schedule plastic surgery. I'm talking about cutting up your credit cards. One woman recently handed me 12 charge cards after worship one weekend, asking me to destroy them. Credit is an addiction! If you have trouble eating too much candy, you don't want to keep the candy dish around. So schedule some plastic surgery and cut up those cards. Isn't it exciting that Jesus came, not to give us one more thing to believe in,

but to liberate us to live as the children of God we were created to be?

Part Three

The Practice
of a
Disciplined
Lifestyle

"Pour oil
into all
the jars..."

Creators vs. Consumers

The wife of a man from the company of the prophets cried out to Elisha, "Your servant my husband is dead, and you know that he revered the Lord. But now his creditor is coming to take my two boys as his slaves."

Elisha replied to her, "How can I help you? Tell me, what do you have in your house?"

"Your servant has nothing there at all," she said, "except a little olive oil."

Elisha said, "Go around and ask all your neighbors for empty jars. Don't ask for just a few. Then go inside and shut the door behind you and your sons. Pour oil into all the jars, and as each is filled, put it to one side."

She left him and shut the door behind her and her sons. They brought the jars to her and she kept pouring. When all the jars were full, she said to her son, "Bring me another one."

But he replied, "There is not a jar left." Then the oil stopped flowing.

She went and told the man of God, and he said, "Go, sell the oil and pay your debts. You and your sons can live on what is left."
— 2 Kings 4:1-7

We all must live with money on the mind, but none of us should live with money on the heart. In a poll of our "global" church family through our website, we asked, "What is your biggest source of concern over money?"

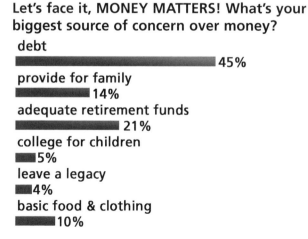

Let's face it, MONEY MATTERS! What's your biggest source of concern over money?

debt
45%
provide for family
14%
adequate retirement funds
21%
college for children
5%
leave a legacy
4%
basic food & clothing
10%

Forty-five percent of the respondents say their number one concern is to get out of debt. The second major concern from the survey is retirement funds. The number three response is providing for family, and number four is basic food and clothing. The fifth highest response is college for children, and the sixth highest response involves leaving a legacy.

Jesus came not only for us to believe in him but also to deliver us from everything that would oppress us. God desires financial freedom for all God's children. Jesus came not only for us to believe in him but also to deliver us from everything that would oppress us. I was taught early in my adult life about how to submit myself to God's laws for financial freedom. Life is so short. Why miss God's best? When young adults are able to start out living under the laws of God, great power can be released through the abundance of God's provision, yet it is never too late for any of us. You were created in God's image, wired to be a creator not a consumer. We must create more than we consume or we cease to exist.

In 2 Kings 4 we read that "The wife of a member of the company of prophets cried to Elisha, 'Your servant my husband is dead.' A single mom who loves God! *"You know your servant revered the LORD, but a creditor has come to take my two sons as slaves."* This was the equivalent of modern day bankruptcy. (Are you mortgaging your children's future today?) *"Now Elisha said to her,* 'What shall I do for you?' Single mom, loves God, in debt, afraid to answer the telephone because the creditors are on her doorstep. *"'Tell me, what do you have in the house?' She answered, 'Your servant has nothing in the house, nothing at all, except for this little jar of olive oil.' He said, 'Go outside; borrow jars from all of your neighbors, empty jars, and not just a few.'"*

What does God want to do in your life? Blessing and abundance—and not just a little. *"Then go in and shut the door behind you and your children. Start pouring oil into all of these jars. When each is full, set it aside." So she left him and shut the door behind her and her chil-*

dren kept bringing jars to her and she kept pouring. When the jars were full she said to her son, "Bring me another jar," but he said to her, "there are no more." They should have trusted God and gotten a few more vessels!

The blessings of God are unlimited. It is only our faith and our lack of willingness to respond fully to what God tells us to do that keeps us from

It is only our faith and our lack of willingness to respond fully to what God tells us to do that keeps us from experiencing the blessings of God.

experiencing the blessings of God. Then the oil stopped flowing. She came and told the man of God and he said, *"Go, sell the oil, pay your debts and you and your children can live on the rest."*

Faithfully Live

Before you can experience what it means to be a creator of life rather than a consumer of life, you must be truly living by faith. The opposite of faith is fear. Fear induces panic, and panic creates impulsive decision-making. The first thing we do when we panic is to go back to the credit card. This widow was in a situation where she panicked and was about to use the last of her resources for the immediate hunger she felt. She was ready to consume instead of create, but financial freedom requires that you create more than you consume. You must make more than you spend. She was about ready to use the last asset she had, and then simply lie down and prepare to die.

Financial freedom requires that you create more than you consume. You must make more than you spend.

Impulsive decision making can lead to bad investments. People who are highly in debt begin to think of getting out of that debt the fastest way possible, and thus become very susceptible to con artists who promise to give a return on money that will never materialize. There are no quick fixes to our unhealthy habits! Who buys lottery tickets? Wealthy people are not buying lottery tickets; it is the poor who cannot afford them. Bad decisions are born when we live out of fear, not out of faith.

When you begin to live in fear and panic, you will be tempted to lose integrity. You will be tempted to do things you don't truly want to do, such as lie, steal, report false income to the government, or write bad checks. Even church people have been known to do such things; however, anytime we step outside the boundaries of God's integrity, God will not prosper us. God will never bless our poor choices.

To truly live is to be free of fear and paralysis. Fear keeps us from making healthy decisions and keeps us in a perpetual cycle of debt and defeat, but I encourage you to hear the word of the Lord. Today is the day of salvation! Today is the day you can experience the power of God to free you from that which binds you up.

Changing Your Character

Notice how the widow came to Elisha with her financial need. She addressed him as "a man of God." She had observed how God had prospered Elisha, how God had blessed him, and now she wanted that blessing herself.

What do you have in your house? After teaching these principles in our congregation, someone wrote me a note, "Can you pay off my debts?" Even if I could have done so, the problem would be that the beneficiary's character had not changed. This person would go directly back into the same indebted situation. God wants to change our character. So, Elisha turned the problem around to the widow, "What do you want me to do for you? It is God who blessed me, like God has blessed you. You are a woman who fears God and loves God." Elisha proposed that the widow take some responsibility by asking, *"What do you have in your house?"*

You already have all the gifts, all the talents, and all the resources you need to build a basis for financial freedom within you. What does he mean? We can imagine the widow crying out, I don't have anything in my house! Obviously, Elisha, you are the one that is blessed. I don't have anything. Look around; there is nothing in my house except this little jar of olive oil!

Now, you who are already in Jesus Christ have all the resources you need for God to produce the miracle that you need in your life. You already have all the gifts, all the talents, and all the resources you need to build a basis for financial freedom within you. God has wired you to be a creator, not a consumer, who is using those talents and resources wisely.

Faithfully Work

As those who are wired to create, each of us is required to work, to faithfully work. What did Elisha commission this woman to do? He did not put her on welfare. You are never going to find a blessing on welfare. Welfare might be a temporary solution, but if continued indefinitely it will only erode esteem and prevent you from discovering what it means to live in dependence upon God, by relying instead on the government.

Unlike any other creature, you have the ability to conceive something in your mind and then put it to work. Elisha challenged this woman to become engaged in the economy. There is a repercussion of sin in our culture that has caused us to believe a distorted premise, that leisure is more valuable than work. We think in our heads that we are going to find ultimate meaning in leisure, so we try to minimize work. We try to work as little as possible, so we can maximize leisure. Our culture is throwing this at us all the time, as encapsulated in the slogan, T.G.I.F. (Thank God It's Friday.) I thank God it's Friday because I can step it up and go to work for God on Saturday and Sunday. We are created to be creative! We must create more than we consume or we cease to exist. Of all the creatures that God created; you are created in the image of God. It doesn't mean that you physically look like God; rather that you also have the ability to create. Unlike any other creature, you have the ability to conceive something in your mind and then put it to work. It will multiply and create more resources in your life than you consume. As long as you are creating, you will thrive. When your consumption becomes greater than your creativity, you will begin to die.

Jesus said you must become like a little child. No one tells a little child to go out to the street and build a lemonade stand. It is in their nature. It is in the nature of children to create and be entrepreneurial. After a snowfall, as children we got out our snow shovels and hit the neighborhood because we knew we would get $3 to $5 for each driveway we shoveled! No one had to tell us to do that. It was something inside us—we were born to create more than we consume.

We are created to be creative. God is going to supply resources through meaningful work that will contribute to other people's needs. Notice that meaningful work is a gift, and we must see our jobs, or seek work, in that light. We thrive best when we are in meaningful work. Maria is a single mom who went through a divorce and found herself wondering how she was going to feed her own children. Here is her version of the 2 Kings story, a powerful example of how God provides:

(Maria) I am a tool and die maker. How I became a tool and die maker was an absolute miracle. I was halfway through life when I found myself single again. I had been married for 21 years and I didn't have a career. I was a stay-at-home mom, so I had to start over. I had to totally start over.

One of the first things that I did was get a six-dollar-an-hour job because any job beat no job. I was filing papers for a mortgage company. I would go home on my lunch hour and look for work. I did a lot of praying. When reading the paper I saw an ad and that is where I found out what a tool and die maker was. I just felt like the Lord led me in that direction. So this one particular company I called two to three times a week for three to four months. I told them I would sweep the floors, pour coffee, drive trucks, shine shoes, telling them that I wanted my little foot inside their door to prove to them that I was willing to work. And they gave me a start.

All total, the first couple of years, I probably put in 60 to 70-hour weeks. I had to go to school, had to study, and I had to learn how to run equipment that I had never seen before in my life. I was well aware that it was a man's world. I was desperate. It was very intimidating. There were some days that I would go home and cry for an hour or two. There were times when I thought about quitting. There were times when I did quit...I just didn't tell anyone, and I got up and went to work the next day.

Now I love going to work, knowing that I can bring a paycheck home and pay all my bills and have money left over. Because of my job I have been able to totally get out of debt. Initially, I was shop help and they then allowed me to become an apprentice and now I am a tool and die maker. I have arrived."[8]

God promises to supply all our needs, and provides resources through meaningful work that will contribute to the needs of others. That is exactly what the widow did; she went into the oil business by using the scant resources she already possessed.

My own situation reflects the same power of God, who used the resources I had. When I came to my congregation, I preached at one worship celebration a week. Soon I wanted to multiply that, so I preached two, then three, then four, using the buildings we had at the time and filling them up, one celebration at a time. Today we experience six celebrations live each weekend and one on video, with plans to start more. Creative opportunity in meaningful work is my blessing. You also are created to be creative.

Benjamin Franklin said, "Sloth like rust consumes faster than labor wears." Proverbs 28:19 said, *"Anyone who tills the land will have plenty of bread,*

---

[8] View Maria's story, "Working Woman" on the DVD within *Money Matters: Financial Freedom For All God's Churches,* or view it at www.ginghamsburg.org/mm.

The first false premise is that leisure is a higher value than work; the second false premise is that older people are less useful and productive.

but one who follows worthless pursuits will have plenty of poverty" (NRSV). The first false premise is that leisure is a higher value than work; the second false premise is that older people are less useful and productive. We have had retirement in this country only since 1930. Retirement was unheard of until a system was put into place. In 1930, a man's life expectancy was fifty-eight and a woman's was sixty-two, so the retirement age was set at sixty-five. It was a semi-arbitrary number, designed to make for a short span between the end of paid employment and death, but it caused a person to think, "Okay—I am expected to retire."

When a person retires, the tendency is to begin to consume more than create, and this mindset often signals the beginning of the end of their life. That is not what God had in mind when God created us! Conversely, older biblical characters such as Moses demonstrated some of the best work around. Moses was eighty before God could even use him effectively. Prior to this, Moses didn't have the maturity it took to influence people; his faith and wisdom arrived late in life. Many great persons have made incredible accomplishments when past their so-called prime:

- Michelangelo painted the Last Judgment on the ceiling of the Sistine Chapel when he was 59.

- P.T. Barnum produced his first circus at the age of 60.

- Colonel Sanders, at age 66, started the Kentucky Fried Chicken chain.

- Ronald Reagan was elected to his first term as president at age 69. He was the oldest person to ever be elected president until he was elected for a second term at 73, taking his age to 78 when he eventually left office.

- Golda Meir became prime minister of Israel at age 71.

- Nelson Mandela, at age 75, became the first black president of South Africa after suffering in jail as a political prisoner for 27 years.

- John Glenn, at age 77, traveled into space for his second time.

- Benjamin Franklin was elected as a delegate to the Constitutional Convention at 81.

- Paul Harvey arises before sunrise every day for the past 84 years and produces a radio program that is heard all over the world.

At any given age, as long as you are creating more than you are consuming you will experience the blessing of God.

Faithfully Invest

Not only must you faithfully work; you must faithfully invest what God has given you through your labor. Look at Elisha's instructions again. "Go outside; borrow jars from all of your neighbors, empty jars, but not just a few." The widow was required to invest the oil she was ready to spend for their last meal. No, don't spend it... invest it. *"Go inside and shut the door behind you and your sons. Pour oil into all the jars, and as each is filled, put it to one side."* You are strongly advised to multiply what God has given you.

What do you have in your house? You may be thinking, "Who is going to help me? I don't have anything... who is going to help me?"

Everything you need you already have. Now you must work the package that God has given you. Do you have Jesus as teacher, guide, and ruler of your life? Then you have the gifts, talents, and resources you need. Everything you need you already have. Now you must work the package that God has given you.

What comes to mind when you are asked, "What are your assets?" Most people immediately begin calculating their material possessions, but an asset is actually something of value that will help you produce income and benefit others. For example, "Jan" has an incredibly pleasant personality and energy. You know those types... the kind of personality that allows her to work part-time at Wal-Mart as a greeter, which enabled her to add $9,000 to her family income last year. Do you know how big of an asset Jan's personality is? Today, you would need $300,000 in a Certificate of Deposit at today's current C.D. interest rates, to provide $9,000 in annual income. Jan's asset is not $300,000 in a C.D.; it is her energy and personality that allows her to make the same money as having $300,000 in a C.D, and she already possesses that personality. If you go into partnership with God, watch the value multiply on the assets that God has given you.

Strategic Partnerships

When setting out to make full use of your assets, you must maximize your potential through strategic partnerships. The first thing that the widow in

2 Kings did was to create a strategic partnership with a person of God who could pull her forward.

I came to my congregation as a local pastor when it was a little country church. It's where the United Methodist denomination sent me, making $8,800 a year. When I came to the congregation, I wanted to learn from the best leaders in Christian ministry, so I went to conferences. I wanted to hang out with the best local pastors in the world. I was 28 years old and flew from Ginghamsburg (Ohio) to Pasadena, California to attend a conference for *large* church pastors. I wanted to hang out with successful people in order to maximize the potential God had placed inside me.

You must maximize your potential by finding strategic partnerships. Look for those persons who are a little ahead of you, or who are gifted in areas that you aren't. I remember standing in Pasadena with a bunch of guys who were probably in their late forties and early fifties. They looked very successful, and there I was in my blue jeans. I had a baby at home and was driving a 1966 Volkswagen, with a six-volt battery. I saw these successful pastors standing in a circle, and as I inched my way over, I heard one of them say, "John, tell me what is happening in your church." John replied, "I don't know. I need you guys to pray for me, for a new vision. Our church has plateaued at 5,000 people on the weekends." I wanted to learn from that pastor because he had not ceased in his desire to be creative! All you need has already been given to you; you must maximize your potential by finding strategic partnerships. Look for those persons who are a little ahead of you, or who are gifted in areas that you aren't. Ask if you can pick their brain, shadow behind them, or meet to discuss your best next steps. Watch God provide as you take these essential steps toward freedom.

This is why we all need to have money on our mind, but none of us should have money on our hearts. Christ's mission must be where our key investments are placed. Here is what the Bible says: *"Honor the LORD with your wealth"* (Proverbs 3:9a). It doesn't matter how much you have. You can take a little of what you have and first invest it in God's mission before you invest in anything else. Giving is an act of worship. The Bible says, *"For where your treasure is there your heart will be also."* This is why we all need to have money on our mind, but none of us should have money on our hearts. *"A generous person will prosper"* (Proverbs 11:25a). No matter how much we have struggled, our family has always written that first 10 percent of whatever we receive to the Lord's work. We have never had any debt, and God has blessed and multiplied.

After you invest in Christ's mission, you must participate in the markets. The woman in 2 Kings was getting into oil futures. You will never make money if you keep it under your mattress or in a bank's savings account. Elisha was saying to this woman that she would need to participate in the fruits of the economy. It is the principle of sowing and reaping. You must take a risk to reap a reward. Any farmer knows that when they put their seed into the ground, they risk losing it if the weather conditions are not right. Sometimes they can be fearful and hesitate to put their seed into the ground because they think the conditions are not right, yet until they risk that seed to the ground, they will never participate in the multiplication of the harvest.

The book, *Wealth to Last*,[9] developed a sequential investing plan, "Five Steps." The first step is completed before going to the second, and so forth. Here are the steps, which I have used:

It All Matters: **Further Steps For** **Freedom Finders**

1. **Eliminate all high-interest and short-term debts.** When you pay off your debt, you are immediately guaranteed a return on your money of 15 percent to 21 percent because that is what you are paying right now in interest. Since this is an immediate return, you want to pay that off first.

2. **Create an emergency fund.** We had several emergencies in our household. First, our air conditioner went out. It had a ten-year guarantee on it, but we've owned the house eleven years, and it cost us $3,000 to repair. Then we had repairs to the outside of our house to fix where moisture got under the siding, another $3,000. Then my car broke down and that was $500 to fix. In no time expenses jumped $7,000. If I did not have an emergency fund, what would I have done? I would have pulled out the plastic. If you have an emergency fund, you are prepared for those emergencies that come up, and you won't get caught in the cycle of debt.

3. **Save toward major purchases** (such as your next car). The best way to do that is in a bank certificate of deposit (C.D.) or government secured mutual fund that allows you to withdraw your money without penalty. Save for a major purchase.

[9] Larry Burkett, Ron Blue, Jeremy White, *Wealth to Last* (Broadman, 2003).

4. Diversify to meet long-term goals. Compound interest is our friend! For our son's college, Carolyn and I threw something into mutual funds every month from the time he was born until fifth grade. Because of commitments to God's mission, from fifth grade on we did not save for college anymore. We had put in $5, $10, and $25 as we went along, and by the time he was in fifth grade we had put $1,000 in his college fund. With mutual funds that became $4,000 by the time he graduated from high school. $1,000 became $4,000 in a very short period of time because we had this mutual fund.

You may be saying, "Wait a minute. I have lost forty percent of my investment since 9/11." Many are in that situation, triggered by a war. Market loss is not the same thing as market fluctuation. If you didn't cash in, you haven't lost anything. Since the 1800s, the market has always come back. It has gone down thirty-one times on an average of every five years. As long as you don't touch it, you have only experienced market fluctuation, not market loss.

5. Invest in higher risk investments after you meet the other four priorities, but make sure that you are diversified. This will allow you to get multiple returns, and just like the widow in 2 Kings, seek out the advice of a wise investment consultant

Your financial future is filled with hope. Remember that you have a heavenly parent who loves you. Here is the commitment that I am asking you to make: Be a kingdom investor, not a cultural consumer. If anything, fortify your determination to not go further into debt, and work a plan to get out of it. Any farmer can tell you not to eat all of your seed.

You must create more than you consume or you cease to exist.

"They all ate and were satisfied."

Chapter Seven

Lifestyles of the Disciplined and Generous

When the apostles returned, they reported to Jesus what they had done. Then he took them with him and they withdrew by themselves to a town called Bethsaida, but the crowds learned about it and followed him. He welcomed them and spoke to them about the kingdom of God, and healed those who needed healing.

Late in the afternoon the Twelve came to him and said, "Send the crowd away so they can go to the surrounding villages and countryside and find food and lodging, because we are in a remote place here."

He replied, "You give them something to eat."

They answered, "We have only five loaves of bread and two fish— unless we go and buy food for this crowd." (About five thousand men were there.)

But he said to his disciples, "Have them sit down in groups of about fifty each." The disciples did so, and everybody sat down. Taking the five loaves and the two fish and looking up to heaven, he gave thanks and broke them. Then he gave them to the disciples to set before the people. They all ate and were satisfied, and the disciples picked up twelve basketfuls of broken pieces that were left over. — Luke 9:10-17

Freedom in any area of life comes from submitting that area to the eternal laws of God. You will always be frustrated in relationships until you submit them to the eternal laws of God. You will always be frustrated in your physical, mental, emotional, and spiritual health until you submit to the laws of God. It's the same with your finances. Financial freedom is found as we exercise God's principle of generous giving.

Generous giving is an expression of your heart, and heart is most closely connected to spirit. Generous giving is an expression of your heart, and heart is most closely connected to spirit. The other practices in this book make sense intellectually. They are principles of the head, such as paying off your high interest, or short-term debt. That makes sense. That's logical. But generous giving is a principle of the heart.

No one wants actually wants to be a Scrooge, especially those who call themselves followers of Jesus. No one wants their tombstone to read, "Here Lies A Tightwad: He went through life with his fist tightly squeezed and withheld doing good at every opportunity." Why is there something in nearly all of us that makes us want to give? Giving is an attitude of the heart. When you live by the Spirit, there's something about giving that "feels right." Contrarily, when you live out of your body or flesh, you do what "feels good." Do you see the difference between righteousness and satisfaction?

If it feels so right to give, why do we struggle? Why is giving so hard? For example, in the year 2000 only eight percent of Americans gave 10 percent of their income (which is a tithe) or more. The average family spends $240 a month on fast food. The average family in America gives five dollars a month to a cause that would help the poor. Why does giving feel so right but is so hard to do?

Luke 9 describes one of two Gospel accounts of Jesus multiplying bread and fish to feed large crowds of people. In the earlier Gospels, Jesus fed 4000 from bread and loaves that the disciples had scrimped together. In the last account (John 6) a child gave up his lunch, and 5000 were fed.

Luke 9:12 tells us that *"The day was drawing to a close and the Twelve came to him and said, 'Send the crowd away so that they may go to the surrounding villages and countryside to lodge and get provisions for we are here in a deserted place.' But he said to them, 'You give them something to eat.'"* Financial freedom results from submitting ourselves to all the laws of God, including

The act of generous giving actually activates the law of miraculous multiplication.

generous giving, but the problem is our mentality that is based in scarcity. The disciples complained by saying that they had only five loaves and two fish, unless they could go into town to buy more. We have a tendency to focus on our limitations and not the limitlessness of God. The act of generous giving actually activates the law of miraculous multiplication.

The Nature of God

"For God so loved the world that he gave his one and only Son, that whoever believes in him shall not perish but have eternal life"—John 3:16. Generosity is the nature of God. God *gave* his only son. You can't have love without generosity. Love, in its purest form, is the act of generous, sacrificial

THE NATURE OF GOD

giving. Most of the time when people talk about love, they actually mean lust, which is selfish consumption rather than sacrificial commitment. Often when I counsel a couple that is getting married, especially persons getting married for the second or third time, I say, "Wait a minute! You've been through this before. Marriage is hard. It is the hardest thing I know. Even when it is good, it's hard." And I'll often hear this response, "No one has ever made me *feel* this way before." What are these romantics thinking about? They are not talking about love; they are not feeling love. They are feeling lust. Lust is not just sexual; rather it exists whenever consumption exceeds generosity. It took me twenty years of marriage to Carolyn before my giving meter exceeded my lust meter, before I really reached that love stage. You do not truly love if there is an absence of generous sacrificial giving.

Lust is not just sexual; rather it exists whenever consumption exceeds generosity.

Giving always honors God and blesses people. We read about Jesus taking the five loaves and two fish. What were the five loaves and two fish? The disciples' lunch! He took the disciples' lunch money!

That is true biblical giving. It will always honor God by making God more visible, and it will always bless other people by providing for their needs.

He then looked up to heaven. Jesus' first gift was to God. He blessed it, divided it, and gave it to the disciples so they could bless people. That is true biblical giving. It will always honor God by making God more visible, and it will always bless other people by providing for their needs.

Some Christians ask me if giving to the United Way or the police boosters is counted in biblical giving. I respond that there is good giving and there is God giving. When the Bible talks about the giving of your resources, it requires two components; it must honor God by making God more visible. Others see it and they think or say what Jesus observed: *"By this everyone will know that you are my disciples, by the way you love one another"* (John 13:35). Biblical giving won't honor you; it will honor God, and secondly it will be a blessing to other people. When I give to the United Way or to the police boosters, it's not counted in my God-giving.

Jesus emphasized *"it is more blessed to give than to receive"* (Acts 20:35).

You never feel better (more "right") than when you are giving in a way that honors God and blesses other people.

Jesus knew and demonstrated that we are most like God when we are giving. It's in that state of righteous generosity that we experience the benefit of endorphins, the euphoric chemicals that are released by the brain into the body. You never feel better (more "right") than when you are giving in a way that honors God and blesses other people.

The Love of God

THE LOVE OF GOD

Generosity is the expression of our love for God. Generous giving is an act of worship. Jesus said, *"For where your treasure is, there your heart will be also"* (Matthew 6:21). Financial freedom is not about the love of money; rather it's the result of the love of God. The Bible says that when you honor God with your wealth, when you make that first priority, everything else in your life will fall into place. Put first the kingdom of God and his righteousness, then everything else will be provided for you. Financial freedom is not about the love of money; it's about the love of God, how you worship and where you put your treasure. The Bible calls this the principle of the tithe.

What exactly is the tithe? Most people, even people who have been in the church for years, don't really understand what a tithe is. Someone says, "Well, I give my tithe to the church, and I'm growing into giving 10 percent." Actually the tithe literally means *the tenth*.

The prophet Malachi called for financial freedom with this challenge,

> *Will anyone rob God? Yet you are robbing me! But you say, "How are we robbing you?" In your tithes and offerings! You are cursed with a curse, for you are robbing me—the whole nation of you! Bring the full tithe into the storehouse, so that there may be food in my house, and thus put me to the test, says the* Lord *of hosts; see if I will not open the windows of heaven for you and pour down for you an overflowing blessing.—Malachi 3:8-10 (NRSV)*

A tithe is the first 10 percent, and an offering is anything above the first 10 percent. That definition is not to discourage the person who has two cents to give. You give what you have, but a tithe is the first 10 percent. "Bring the full tithe into the storehouse." What is the storehouse? At the time of this writing by the prophet, it was the Temple. Then it became the synagogue in the Jewish tradition, and for Christians, the house of worship is our church. Bring the full tithe into the storehouse so there may be food in

We can do more together as faith communities to honor God and bless others than any of us could do alone. the house for the economy of God. Why is that so strategic? Because we can do more together as faith communities to honor God and bless others than any of us could do alone. We are able to extend our reach towards the needs of the poor, hurting, and oppressed as the body of Christ much further than we could individually do by ourselves. When everyone does their part and brings their full tithe into the storehouse, there won't be a need for anyone to say, "We must raise $60 here for outreach and $17,000 there for building maintenance" because it will already be in the storehouse.

"Put me to the test, says the LORD of hosts; see if I will not open the windows of heaven for you and pour down for you an overflowing blessing." What opens the floodgates of heaven? What releases the "law of miraculous provision," such as we see with the loaves and fish? Our tithes and offerings open the floodgates of heaven when we live out the law of generous giving.

The Provision of God

Generous giving is an act of faith. What did the disciples do before God could take their resources and miraculously multiply? They let go of them! What's the hardest thing for us to do? If I give my lunch money to you, how am I going to have lunch? Isn't that the issue right here? Jesus is not going to make something from nothing. Did you know that 10,000 children in the world *today* died from starvation? We lament, "Oh, why isn't God helping the babies?" Jesus isn't going to do something from nothing. Jesus needs your lunch. You must risk trusting God with what you have, and that's why

Jesus isn't going to do something from nothing. Jesus needs your lunch.

giving is an act of worship. You can say you believe in God, but you don't trust God until you put faith into action.

There is a difference between believing God and trusting God. We must trust God with what we've been given. Timothy calls us to, *"Command those who are rich in this world not to be arrogant nor to put their hope in wealth, which is so uncertain, but to put their hope in God, who richly provides us with everything for our enjoyment"* (1 Timothy 6:17). You must release what God has given you; you must open your hand. When you

God loves you, but God doesn't trust you until you show you are worthy of God's trust. release it, when you put what you've got in God's hand, guess what? You're saying to God, "I trust you." Now guess what God can say? God can trust you too. God loves you, but God doesn't trust you until you show you are worthy of God's trust. Since God loves you unconditionally, you don't have to do a thing to earn God's love, but you must do something to earn God's trust.

When you demonstrate that you trust God, things start to happen. Jesus blessed the bread, he broke it, and then to whom did he give it? Back to the disciples! When they got it back, was it the same quantity? No, it was multiplied enough to feed thousands. And at the end, after everyone else was fed, the disciples collected twelve baskets of leftovers! When we are generous, we set the "law of miraculous multiplication" into effect in our lives. We can become God's means of provision in the lives of other people. When we continue to bless other people, God blesses us more so that we can continue to bless more people.

When we continue to bless other people, God blesses us more so that we can continue to bless more people.

God astonishes us because what we give doesn't come back in the same quantity. It's like a yo-yo. You can't really get rid of this thing, yet it comes back in a larger quantity that when it left. Jesus says, *"Give and it will be given to you. A good measure, pressed down, shaken together and running over, will be poured in your lap. For the measure you give will be the measure you get back"* (Luke 6:38 NRSV). We find the same idea in 2 Corinthians 9:6, *"Whoever sows sparingly will also reap sparingly, and whoever sows generously will also reap generously."* The poor have a place of prominence for God's blessing. It is why God will hold us accountable as a people if we spend our resources building fancy sanctuaries rather than investing our money into the real needs of people.

Freedom Finders

Further Steps For

It All Matters:

1. **Set aside money for giving.** The very first thing we must do is to give. It's an act of faith, not an act of logic. Eliminating high interest and short-term debt makes sense, but the first thing we do should come not out of sense-making but out of faith-making logic. In 1 Corinthians 16:2 the apostle Paul said, *"On the first day of every week, each one of you should set aside a sum of money in keeping with your income, saving it up, so that when I come no collections will have to be made."* This is called *planned giving* or *giving on purpose.* It's about intentionally committing to set aside an amount of money to give to God's purpose.

2. **Discipline yourself in giving.** Second Corinthians 8:6 calls us to *"bring also to completion this act of grace on your part,"* so do it! Finish it. Don't just say that is a good idea, only to do whatever "feels good" rather than what "feels right." Living by the Spirit means doing the right thing; not the self-satisfying or easy thing. Live by the Spirit and exceed the limits of your comfort zone. A mountain climber puts metal stakes in the rock as he or she climbs. Even if the climber slips, they can never fall back farther than their last stake. So every year, set a stake and build layer upon layer so you never fall below your last commitment.

3. **Base your plan upon God's promises.** When you think about giving and specifically when you make a commitment to give, don't focus on your limitations; focus on God's limitlessness. Kiss the scarcity mindset good-by. Make your commitment by faith. Keep your focus on Jesus. Here's the promise of Deuteronomy 15:10: *"Give generously and the LORD your God will bless you in all your work and in all you undertake."* What a promise! How will you express your love and trust back to God?

A Call to Action:

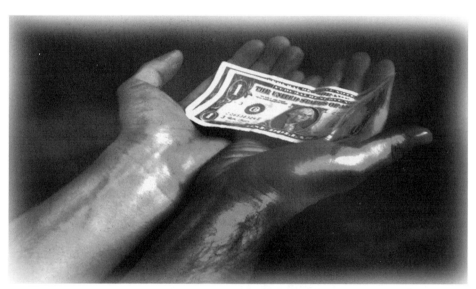

The Power of Ultimate Sacrifice

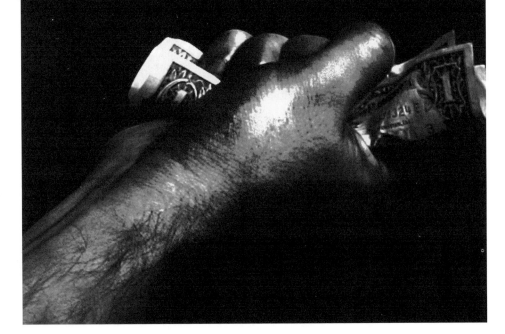

"What does it profit them if they gain the whole world but lose themselves?"

A Call to Action

If any want to become my followers, let them deny themselves and take up their cross daily and follow me. For those who want to save their life will lose it, and those who lose their life for my sake will save it. What does it profit them if they gain the whole world, but lose or forfeit themselves?— Jesus, from Luke 9:23-25 (NRSV)

Each day as I look at God's word, I continue to ask myself, "Am I the real deal, or am I settling for something less? Am I the real deal or could I be accepting an institutional religion that human beings have created, rather than becoming the authentic follower that Jesus has called me to be?" Have you ever asked yourself this question?

Here is a prayer you may want to say as you sum up what you have learned about money:

Lord Jesus, sometimes I hear Your words but they never really get past my ears. Sometimes I even believe I get it and yet I still buy into the materialistic values of the world around me. So Lord, in the presence of the Holy Spirit I pray that You do a deeper work in my life. Cut past my phoniness and my excuses. I pray this in Jesus' name, Amen.

Spending Habits

There is no better gauge of our priorities and values than the way we spend money. It reveals all kinds of things about us. The way we deal with money is really the window to our worldview. Jesus said people come from two different places. The majority—and this includes the majority of people in the church today—pour their passion into the pursuit of building treasures on earth, treasures that have no permanence. Whatever we spend our energy on that will not live past the grave is a waste of time. Many of us are in debt, paying for things we no longer even have, things that long ago wore out. If you pour yourself into the pursuit of acquiring worldly things—if that is your primary goal, what your energy is going toward, and where you are accruing debt— you need to hear clearly that there is no permanence in worldly things. Jesus said that very few people will passionately pursue building treasure in heaven. *"But small is the gate and narrow the road that leads to life, and only a few find it"* (Matthew 7:14).

> **There is no better gauge of our priorities and values than the way we spend money.**

Financial freedom ultimately comes down to the trust of sacrifice. Luke 9:23 is the passage I wrestle with when asking myself if I'm the real deal or settling for something less. More than mere words in a book; this passage represents the very call of Jesus. *"If any want to become my followers, let them deny themselves and take up their cross daily and follow me. For those who want to save their life will lose it, and those who lose their life for my sake will save it. What does it profit them if they gain the whole world, but lose or forfeit themselves?"*

The Cost of the Cross

My purpose is not to help you do better financially so that **Everything about life, everything about the purpose of God in our life, returns to this cost of the cross.** you can go away and merely be blessed. My intent is to challenge your own worldview against the worldview of the Lord Jesus Christ. Everything about life, everything about the purpose of God in our life keeps coming back to this cost of the cross.

Mel Gibson's depiction of Christ's final days caused more conversation and controversy than any movie I am aware of in the last decade. *The Passion of the Christ* showed what the reality of the cross is all about, that it is not merely a religious icon. It fleshes out what the prophet Isaiah said about the coming of the Messiah, several hundred years before Jesus was born.

> *He was despised and rejected by others;*
> *a man of suffering and acquainted with infirmity;*
> *and as one from whom others hide their faces*
> *he was despised, and we held him of no account.*
>
> *Surely he has borne our infirmities*
> *and carried our diseases;*
> *yet we accounted him stricken,*
> *struck down by God, and afflicted.*
>
> *But he was wounded for our transgressions,*
> *crushed for our iniquities;*
> *upon him was the punishment that made us whole,*
> *and by his bruises we are healed.*
>
> *All we like sheep have gone astray;*
> *we have all turned to our own way,*

*And the LORD has laid on him
the iniquity of us all.*

*He was oppressed, and he was afflicted,
yet he did not open his mouth;
like a lamb that is led to the slaughter,
and like a sheep that before its shearers is silent,
so he did not open his mouth. —Isaiah 53:3-7 (NRSV)*

Through the years many merchants have reduced the cross to a piece of art. We have reduced it again to a fashionable piece of silver or gold. Didn't someone once betray Jesus with several pieces of silver? Jesus, as God in the flesh, demonstrated that life is not about self. Jesus' brand of humility (Philippians 2:6-11) was a powerful statement, proving that he did not come to earth to pursue his personal gratification.

God won't say, "Well, what did you buy?"

Look at us on the other hand. We run around doing everything we want, taking care of our own needs. Debt results as we go about pursuing our own desires. Jesus knew life wasn't about getting what he wanted and doing his own thing. His purpose was clearly to carry out the mission and purpose of God. God has not placed us here to consume. When we sit before the God on Judgment Day, which we will all do, God won't say, "Well, what did you buy?" We are here to live and give to God's purpose and priority. The meaning of life is found in sacrifice.

The Call to Commitment

The opposite of the Christian worldview is the belief and practice that the meaning of life is found in the experience of obtaining satisfaction "right now." Jesus said it is not about immediate self-gratification; it is about your ability to practice discipline right now! It is about your ability to delay gratification right now. This is what Jesus means in Luke 9:24: *"For those who want to save their life will lose it, and those who lose their life for my sake will save it."* You can't lose your life for Jesus and still keep your hand on it. Many of us want to say we are committed, but to be committed means that you relinquish who you are and what you have to God. I didn't say "to believe"; I said "to be committed." Many persons who believe think they are committed. No, you are not committed until you let go and relinquish who you are and what you have to God. Your acts of mercy must match up with your acts of piety.

You are not committed until you let go and relinquish who you are and what you have to God. Baptism defines this commitment. Baptism literally means dead, buried, and out of the way. It is no longer I who live; it is no longer my wants, my preferences, my agenda, or my thirst, but the purpose and Spirit of Christ who lives through me.

Jesus said, *"Unless a kernel of wheat falls to the ground and dies, it remains only a single seed. But if it dies, it produces many seeds"* (John 12:24). If I take out a twenty-dollar bill from my pocket and hang on to it, that twenty-dollar bill will have a very short shelf life. It will most probably turn into a dozen golf balls that would be quickly lost. Or, while going through the airport I'll pick up an American Iron magazine (for people who love Harley Davidsons motorcycles) and spend five dollars for something that I'll leave in the hotel room. If I hang onto a twenty-dollar bill it will have a very short shelf life; The bizarre truth is that as we go through life, we hang on to those twenty-dollar bills, picking up golf balls and magazines, items from which legacies are not born.

If I "plant" that twenty-dollar bill and let it go for God's purposes, however, it grows. Every week Carolyn and I practice a tithe and more... and together with our church family see the effects of our giving grow. In one month's time, New Path, the outreach arm of our congregation served 5,300 families, which is over 17,520 persons. Forty-eight cars were distributed to families needing transportation. The furniture ministry assisted 364 families. Clothing assistance was given to 521 families. Rent and utility help went to 208 families. We are talking about one little piece of paper that comes out of my pocket that could have been a dozen golf balls. If I hang on to it, it has a very short shelf life, but if I release it in community with others, God's love is multiplied among thousands.

Releasing and Resurrection

Here is what I am learning. When I release that twenty-dollar bill, and if I also pay myself through investing, then God will increase the wealth of my seed for the purpose of blessing others. As long as I hang on to this bill, it is not going to become anything but twelve golf balls or a magazine that will be discarded tomorrow afternoon. When I release it, it grows. When I invest more, it increases, as God trusts me to bless other people.

Resurrection in any area of your life always comes out of sacrifice. Resurrection in any area of your life always comes out of sacrifice. As long as you are donating and not sacrificing, all you are going to get is religion, but religion has no power. You don't want religion; you want resurrection. Resurrection never happens without the cross, however. As long as you are only donating to the purpose of God, you will never know the power of God in your life.

You now see why I ask myself if I am doing the real deal, or if I have fallen for some institutional, religious human invention. The call of Jesus is a call to follow. Luke 9:23 advises, *"If any want to become my followers* (you notice he doesn't use the word *believers*), *let them deny themselves and take up their cross daily."* It is a practice of sacrifice every day. This Jesus thing is something much bigger than belief. It is about following Jesus in the demonstration of sacrifice.

Bass Boats and Delayed Gratification

Money demonstrates the priority of your values. Wherever you are spending your money, and whatever you are doing with your money tells what you really believe. I have always had a wish list on the side, and a few wishes remain unfulfilled. Many years ago my wish list had a bass boat. It had been on my list for about eight years, from a stage of my life when I was into fishing. Have you noticed as you get to certain stages you go through different desires? I was into fishing, and I would take my kids fishing. It was one of the bonding experiences we had. We were the ones always standing on the bank, and we would see people ride by in their bass boats. I would say to my kids, "Someday Dad is going to get a bass boat." One day I was driving down the expressway with Jonathan and we passed a guy pulling a nice bass boat. So he looked over and said, "Dad, when are we going to get our bass boat?" I looked at him and said, "Jonathan, every year we give a bass boat and more to the church." He never asked me that question again.

Recreation in your life should never precede or exceed God's mission. Why do I have a wish list with things that take me a long time to get? Delayed gratification. Ironically, if it takes long enough to get something, you often forget why you wanted it in the first place, and that is a good thing.

A lot of people are paying $500 a month for an RV or a boat that gets used four times a year. If what you are spending on recreation exceeds what you are releasing to the mission of Christ, you might believe in Jesus, but you are not following Jesus. Don't forget that every spending decision is a spiritual decision. This doesn't mean you'll never get anything. I saved for years for a Harley motorcycle, on my wish list. I paid cash because you should never ever pay interest on a toy. I went to motorcycle safety school

If your recreation precedes or exceeds what you are releasing to the mission of Christ, you might believe in Jesus, but you are not following Jesus.

and took the classes. I got my license, and I ordered a Harley. But please understand that our family will give much more than that Harley to God's purposes this year.

If your recreation precedes or exceeds what you are releasing to the mission of Christ, you might believe in Jesus, but you are not following Jesus. Jesus said it is hard for a rich person to enter the kingdom of heaven. You see why every spending decision is a spiritual decision, because you are influencing or infecting your children by the values and priorities of what you are doing with your money. What it all comes down to is not what we believe but our commitment to the Lordship of Jesus Christ.

A Fearless Inventory

Do a fearless inventory in your money matters. What you are doing with your money is the true test of your faith. It is why Jesus said, *"Where your treasure is, there your heart is also."* It all comes down to this: it's not whether I believe in God's love but whether I trust God's love. Do I trust God's promise of provision and recognize God's ownership? The earth and all it contains belongs to the Lord, not just the ten percent that I tithe, but everything I have. My talent belongs to God; my ability to produce and to make money belongs to God. Where does that all come from? Everything I have belongs to God and if I recognize that ownership I am releasing to Jesus' Lordship.

I believe that the most important thing we can do as a physical demonstration is to make a commitment. When we do not take the time to sit down and make a commitment, we procrastinate. Procrastination is the great robber of life. I talk to so many people about how they've been convicted in their hearts to do something with their debt. Later, when I ask how they are doing, I see procrastination has robbed them of another year of life.

Commitment happens when you discern what God is asking you to give and then act on God's directive. There is a difference between deciding and discerning. Discernment is asking God what to give. Do what God is blessing, rather than asking God to bless what you are doing. It is not until you release something from your hand that God can trust you with more. May God richly bless your steps into financial freedom.

The most important thing we can do as a physical demonstration is to make a commitment

Prayer of Commitment

Lord, I thank You again for Your persistent love and acceptance and Your patience in my life. You have not deemed that some people in this world should have more than others. You desire blessing for all of Your children, and Lord I want to be a part of that blessing. All around the world people are starving; they are starving physically and spiritually. They need to hear Your word to be liberated, and we want to be a part of what You are going to do. So, Lord, right now I discern Your will and Your word to do what You are blessing. In the name of Jesus I pray, Amen.

It All Matters: **Further Steps For** **Freedom Finders**

1. **Just as Jesus exemplified on the cross, resurrection in any area of your life always comes out of sacrifice.** Name a specific area in your life that currently requires resurrection. What is the sacrifice you will make in order to allow God to be the powerful Life-giver?

2. **Recreation in your life should never precede or exceed God's mission.** How is your ability to practice "delayed gratification"? When have you purchased something you did not need, only to rob yourself and God of something much more long-lasting and significant?

3. **The most important thing we can do as a physical demonstration is to make a commitment.** Follow through all the steps necessary for you to find financial freedom, and make a specific financial commitment to your faith community (storehouse) today.

Finding financial freedom as a child of God is a powerful conversion experience. "So if the Son sets you free, you will be free indeed" (John 8:36). More powerful yet, however, are the exponential results when entire faith communities are transformed financially. Money matters for all God's churches! When entire congregations are financially freed up to reach out with a mission mindset, God is honored, people are blessed, and true kingdom work can begin. No longer a fortress of self-protection, the Church is empowered to move out as a force of health and salvation, to reach the lost and set the oppressed free.

For Further Participation

Tell your pastor about this book that you are reading, as well as the leader's book, *Money Matters: Financial Freedom For All God's Churches* (ISBN 0687495555), a companion guide for leading congregations through a strategic stewardship series. This leader's guide includes insights from Mike Slaughter, as well as an implementation program for a stewardship series. The leader's guide offers worship celebration scripts, sample copies of all communication pieces, and powerful messages for moving your congregation forward. Also included are outlines for group study and classes for dealing with debt. This book, which includes the integrated DVD, featuring stories of financial freedom, is available from Abingdon Press.